SITTING ON THE WALL

A memoir of 1960s seaside holidays in Kilkee, West Clare

Written with affection for Kilkee and its people, with gratitude to the friends I made there, and to all whom I met there, and with love and thanks to Rosie and Patrick - who ensured that the happy and blessed life which the Kilkee days of my youth foretold came to pass in reality.

OUR NEAREST FARAWAY PLACE

Kilkee is a small seaside town lying on the west coast of County Clare, on Ireland's Atlantic seaboard.

It is built round a sandy, horseshoe bay. At either end, high cliffs stretch out towards north Clare and the Burren, and out along the Loop Head Peninsula – Corca Baiscinn - to the mouth of the Shannon Estuary.

Since the early nineteenth century, it has been a popular holiday destination, and continues to attract visitors from all over the world – for its stunning scenery, its crystal clear diving waters, and the bracing clean air, driven all the way across the Atlantic from the "next parish" in America. It is a place to relax and, in the truest sense of the word, to re-create oneself.

I first visited Kilkee on Thursday, August 4th 1966 – and the fact that I can pinpoint the exact date gives a clue to how important the town became to me.

Over the following decade in Kilkee, I enjoyed a type of seaside holiday which has all but disappeared now – and, so that it can be remembered, I wanted to recall those days in some detail – the places, the people, the activities – some fifty years after I first encountered "the Queen of the West".

In 1970, an English friend, who I had met at Kilkee's Hydro Hotel, sent me a record – a Beach Boys' single, it was: – "Cottonfields"; and in her accompanying note she said she had sent it because of the instrumental on the B side, called "The Nearest Faraway Place".

"After all," she wrote, "Kilkee *is* our "Nearest Faraway Place".

I thought then, as I do now, that was a good description of the mix of emotions the town stirs up in me. It is familiar, yet engagingly different; it feels like home, yet it was always good to go there, to escape the everyday routines. It evokes a contradiction of feelings, which were all set in motion way back in 1966, when, as a fourteen year old, I first set eyes on Moore Bay, and the town which surrounds it.

The town, and this writer, have changed in the past half century, for better - and for worse, I suspect, but my love for the place and its people has remained consistent.

I wanted to record that love affair; to try and explain how a town can come to mean so much, and to share my memories with those who were there, and with those who still walk on the strand, wander down O'Curry St, or climb the heights of Lookout Hill and give thanks that they know Kilkee - in all its wild beauty, and peaceful solace, as well as in its crazier moments!

I hope these memories, written honestly, and with huge affection, can pay some kind of tribute to the town and its people, and to the many who are no longer with us, who have helped make my life – in Kilkee and elsewhere – such a fortunate, positive, and uplifting experience.

In addition, I think of all those, who, like me, found peace, joy, comfort and excitement in Kilkee – as children, teenagers, or adults, or with parents, siblings, children, friends or partners: those people, of all ages, temperaments, and backgrounds, who hold Kilkee in their hearts, and are thankful for having known the place – for however long, and for whatever reason.

We form a community in all parts of the world; we are the people who gaze up at a high blue sky with scudding clouds, who close our eyes to a warm sea breeze, who breathe in fresh ocean air, and who say to ourselves, and to nobody else in particular: "Ah – it's a Kilkee day."

And I thank any Kilkee residents who will read these words. I thank them for their welcome, their acceptance, and their forebearance, when, in so many different times, and in so many different ways, as an outsider, I tried to tell them what they already knew about their beloved home place.

I never intended to be patronising or glib, no more than I mean to insult or annoy with anything I may write in the pages which follow. Like your town, you have always been special to me, and fifty years has not dimmed my affection in any way.

I daresay I will have made statements in this memoir which some may find inaccurate, misremembered, or, sadly, unwelcome. I can only repeat that it is written with the greatest of good intentions, and based on a genuine love, respect, and admiration for the people of the town and the surrounding areas.

To the many local historians, to the memory of Tim McInerney, to Paddy Nolan, Tom Byrne, J.J. Hickie, and to those whose names I do not know, to the members of Kilkee Civic Trust – I apologise if I have appropriated your stories or research, and, in particular, if I have made errors of history or fact. The fault is all my own. I have tried to acknowledge sources where possible.

It is to all of them this memoir is dedicated – with gratitude, love, friendship and an abiding admiration. For, if Kilkee is wonderful – and it is – then that is down to the efforts of its people for the past two centuries, the welcome they give to visitors, and the fierce pride they have in their town.

I am never sure whether I found Kilkee, or Kilkee found me.

I am just eternally grateful that it happened.

AT FIRST SIGHT

I first set eyes on Kilkee at the beginning of August in 1966 – half a century ago. Time – and life – has progressed since then; Kilkee itself – and the manner in which people holiday there – has changed too – but my love of the place has scarcely dimmed in the five decades since my arrival in the town, as a fourteen year old.

Some background might be helpful, so that the reader can gain an impression of what life experience I was bringing with me.

My mother was widowed when I was five, and, as I was an only child, I think she felt that sharing exciting holidays together might be some kind of compensation for the loss of my father.

She was in love with travel herself. As a nineteen year old, in 1936, she had travelled to Belgium, in possession of detailed instructions on how to locate the farmhouse where her father had been stationed as a gunner during the Battle of Paschendaele. She had also visited a penpal in Holland – a friendship which lasted from schooldays for the rest of her life.

So, in the seven or eight years before I travelled to Kilkee, we had visited most countries in western Europe: France, Italy, Spain, Portugal, Switzerland, Austria, Germany, Holland. This was a time before package holidays, when most folk on our family income would not have been as fortunate, or as widely travelled. I was lucky, as I now acknowledge, that my mother both loved travelling and understood its impact on the young. Of course, as a young child, though excited by the holidays, I just accepted the privilege as "normal".

Interestingly, one of our first trips had been for a summer seaside holiday in Ireland – in Arklow, Co Wicklow; my first visit to my family's country. I was very young at the time, maybe seven years of age – but I remember a cold swimming pool, meals round a big table in the guest house, and, at the start of the holiday, walking along Dublin's O'Connell St past Eason's, on our way to catch the train, and asking my mother how would we be able to understand people speaking to us in Irish.

That is a good reflection of my upbringing and our family's relationship with Ireland.

I knew, from an early age that my dad's father was from Drumkeerin, Co Leitrim and his mother was from Boyle, Co Roscommon. I was aware, too, that my mother's family were Liverpool Irish, with origins in Dundrum and Belfast – but my early childhood was not perhaps typical of an emigrant background. We listened to RTE News each lunchtime in our west Lancashire home, and I was aware of the lyrics of a few rebel songs – but we were not part of an "Irish community" in any sense of the word – there were no dancing or language classes for me, nor was there mention of the GAA or traditional Irish music to any extent. As I had been born in Edinburgh and now lived near Liverpool, maybe my mother thought my origins were confused enough already!

Her experiences when young had been far more related to Ireland – with dances at the Liverpool Irish Centre, membership of the Gaelic League, and frequent visits to Ireland as a young woman – sometimes on holiday, sometimes on Legion of Mary business to work with the organisation's founder, Frank Duff. She had particularly fond memories of Glengarriff in west Cork, and was actually in Howth in September 1939 when war broke out. She had the choice of remaining in Ireland, "for the duration", or returning to Liverpool to be with her family. Her choice was to go home, and she was rewarded with the "May Blitz" and the heavy bombing of her native city over the next four or five years.

As was often the case in those days, her social circle was largely concentrated on church activities, and in the Liverpool of the time, this meant she was friendly with many Irish families, and also with a number of Irish priests – some of whom, on being ordained, had been sent across to the "English Mission" – to serve in archdioceses where priests were in short supply.

One such priest was a Fr Bernard Keating, ordained at All Hallows College, who, as Brian O Céitin, had grown up in what was then the Irish speaking tip of Corca Baiscinn, the Loop Head peninsula, in Kilbaha. As a young curate he had performed the marriage ceremony for my mother's sister, and become a family friend.

Through the years he had continually suggested to my mother that she would enjoy a holiday in this town called "Kilkee" near his homeplace – first as a young single woman, then as a wife and mother, and, eventually, as a widow. The longevity and persistence of his suggestions surely indicated that Kilkee was a place for all ages and situations.

Thankfully, she must have decided, when I reached fourteen years of age, that I was ready to enjoy and appreciate an Irish holiday. I am forever grateful to Fr Barney for repeatedly suggesting Kilkee as a holiday place – and I make sure to visit his grave before the Church of the Little Ark in Moneen on every visit.

So, that was the background to my eventually reaching Kilkee in 1966.

Part of my motivation in writing this account is to outline, to current generations, how different the world was in Kilkee in the 60s – and that would begin with our journey from the north of England to west Clare.

These days that journey would be relatively painless: motorway to Manchester Airport, budget flight to Shannon, hire car to Kilkee with good infrastructure and roads - at least as far as Ennis. With following winds and good luck, it would take less than six hours door to door. In the seventies, when I travelled to Kilkee as a student, via Liverpool to Dublin overnight ferry, and hitch hiking across the country from a point out by Saggart, it could take over twenty hours – again with good luck.

For certain, back in the mid sixties, it was an altogether more sedate affair.

A taxi took us the 50 miles or so to what was then Ringway Airport, Manchester. The entire journey was made on country roads; it took around two hours.

At Ringway we took an Aer Lingus flight to Collinstown, Dublin, and then linked up with a flight to Shannon. Dublin to Shannon flights were more common then, because, with the requirement for transatlantic flights to use Shannon, there were Dublin flights providing a service to join US flights at Shannon – or which were even the first leg of flights to the USA.

Despite its transatlantic gateway status, Shannon was a small airport then, with little security and an easy going feel to it.

10

We were met by a Kilkee taxi driver, supplied by the Hydro Hotel, where we would be staying.

I suppose this was our first piece of luck.

P.J. King, who would later become postmaster at Lisdeen, was a lovely man – keen to introduce us to west Clare, and a fount of local knowledge.

We drove the country roads - no duel carriageways then – in his taxi – and he told us about the places we were passing through.

P.J. didn't have what you might call "the blarney"; there was no smooth running commentary, but, as we passed through Newmarket on Fergus, Clarecastle, and Ennis, he would mention things he knew about the places we were going through. A Coca Cola could cost you ten shillings at the Dromoland Castle Hotel, the turf fire at Fanny O'Dea's in Lissycasey was reputed to have been lit continuously since 1790, when High Court Judge, Lord Norbury was so impressed by the warmth of the inn (and no doubt the famous Egg Flips) on a miserable night, that he awarded them a liquor license on condition that the fire was always lit to welcome travellers.

As I've mentioned, I was well used to seeing different landscapes, despite my young years. I had seen the sun scorched fields of Spain and Portugal, the lush hillsides of the south of France, the polders of Holland, and the mountains of Switzerland and Austria. However, the fields which lay either side of the car as we motored along the switchback of the Ennis to Kilrush mail road – straight, bumpy, and undulating – were a new experience.

There was greenery, and hedges, cattle, and pastel coloured cottages, often next to modern styled bungalows. It was, and it wasn't, familiar. I liked it, though I did start to wonder how far west you could travel without reaching the Atlantic.

The small things I noticed on that first trip were the things I would notice for the rest of my life on that road. Shops and pubs laid back from the road with names on them like J.J. O'Sullivan and Tom Pyne. There was a new modern National School at Lissycasey, and sign posts to places like Ballynacally, Cranny, Kilmurry-McMahon. The signposts were bi-lingual and the road signs different to those at home, and there were an unusual number of slowly driven black or brown Morris Minors, often with trailers, and we frequently passed old bicycles, ridden by women in dresses and cardigans, or men, who inevitably wore dark suits and caps. There were churns left on platforms at crossroads and, a couple of times, we passed two wheeled carts pulled by asses, with twin creamery churns, and nonchalant farmers who looked like they were on automatic pilot. There were a lot of people, who would always acknowledge passers by, with a nod of the head or a raise of the hand, but the road wasn't busy.

It was long before Bord Fáilte had mastered the art of marketing "quaint" Ireland, so I took at face value what I was seeing. The countryside did not seem particularly poor or old fashioned, it was recognisable without being familiar. Without knowing it, I was already becoming comfortable in Ireland.

Eventually we reached Kilrush, and passed the Christian Brothers' School up on the hill to our right – an involuntary shudder from me there, as I was taught at home by the self same order. We climbed the hill out of the town and P.J. assured us it would not be far now.

Here the country was different:, flatter with a bigger sky – it felt like we were getting to the edge of something. As we passed through Moyasta and Tayor's pub, P.J. announced we were half way to Kilkee from Kilrush.

I was getting excited – I loved my holidays and we were about to see our destination. The tiredness of an early start left me, and I strained ahead to see if I could catch sight of Kilkee.

Soon enough there was the bulk of the Atlantic Hotel to the right and the barn like roof of the modern church to the left. The road was straight and I swear P.J. speeded up the car as we approached the sign saying "Cill Chaoidhe".

Of course, I would love to be able to report that it was love at very first sight for Kilkee and me – but that would not be true exactly.

I tried to see the sea as we entered the town, but as we passed down O'Curry St, the shops, windows, and houses all merged into each other, and as we drove towards the West End I was on the wrong side of the car to see over the sea wall.

At the West End Stores we turned up the hill and P.J. parked the taxi outside of the Hydro Hotel. White with red window frames and a tower at one end, with a tricolour and a Clare flag flying, it looked, as I suppose was meant, like a ship at anchor.

We walked in through the doors and into the hotel itself. My first impression was that it was compact. The Reception desk ahead of us was barely wide enough for one person. To my left was a long lounge – divided into two levels with three steps at the half way point. There was a piano at the far end of the room, and chairs and tables all around. People were sitting, chatting quietly or reading, some had pots of tea and plates before them. It was busy without being noisy, comfortable without being prim.

My mother was allocated Room 29 – top floor with a view out over the hotel gardens to the bay. I would say she was also pleased that it afforded her a view of the front door so she could see who was coming and going!

I was in number 31, first floor at the top of the stairs. It had no view, but I came to love it for its convenience to the ground floor. Afterwards, we always had those same rooms – part of the comfort of familiarity which Kilkee holidays provided.

At our evening meal, we sat looking out at the bay. Tired with travel, I did not quite know what to make of this new holiday place.

Outside, there was a steady rain falling, occasionally blustered against the windows by an inconsistent breeze. Nobody was on the strand below. Beneath a gunmetal grey sky, and with the tide at its lowest, the horseshoe bay seemed no more than an expanse of flat mud. Until now I had associated Summer holidays with warmth and sun.

What was this place I had come to?

WHAT WAS THIS PLACE?

If I am to describe to the reader what Kilkee was like in the 1960s, I should probably spend some time considering how Kilkee came to exist in the first place.

I cannot lay claim to great academic accuracy on this subject. There have been excellent pieces of well-researched writing on the origins of Kilkee, and local historians like Tom Byrne, Paddy Nolan, and even the long serving Town Clerk, Timmy McInerney, have contributed to the body of knowledge on the town's history. The Kilkee Civic Trust and the folk at Clare County Library and Kilkee's own Cultúrlann Sweeney also promote the history of the town and its people. However, in keeping with the rather subjective nature of my approach, I can only recount what I have heard and what I believe about the growth and development of Cill Chaoidhe (The church of the lament for St Ita).

On the remote peninsula of Corca Baiscinn, in medieval times, farming and fishing would have been the only sure means of survival. Later, the MacSweeneys and then the MacDonnells were the major landowners. Then the Coyningham family, of Slane Castle in Co Meath, owned the land on which the east end of Kilkee was built – and were responsible for a major rebuilding of the town in 1865. This created the market square, Circular Rd, and a series of wide streets with bow windowed houses which gave part of Kilkee the appearance of an "estate town". The MacDonnell's hailed from Antrim, and the Coyningham's, originally, from Mount Charles in Donegal (hence

Mount Charles Terrace in the town today). Kilkee was popular with northerners in the sixties and I often wondered if they felt some affinity with the town's original landlords!

However, I get ahead of myself.

The remoteness of what we now know as the Loop Head peninsula meant that, a thousand years ago, hermits and holy figures were attracted to the area, as evidenced by the number of holy wells, shrines, and monastic remains.

In later times, however, for the ordinary folk toiling on the land to give profit to the gentry, it must have been little better than subsistence farming. It's fair to surmise that the attractions of the sea's yield, as an alternative to farming the land, would have drawn a fair number of locals. Seaweed has long been used as fertiliser, and even as food in hard times. It would have been a short step over the years to move from farming the seashore to farming the sea itself – especially if the resulting catch fed the family or provided profit for self rather than landlord.

It is not surprising that some would have preferred to risk the "perils of the sea" to feed their families. Equally predictable is the fact that a fishing hamlet would grow around what we now know as Kilkee.

A constant in the development of Kilkee – or indeed its existence at all – is its location. Whether as a fishing village, a Victorian seaside resort, or a modern tourist destination, all of its success and attraction is underpinned by where it is situated

Moore Bay is sheltered – by cliffs on two sides and by the Duggerna Reef which is strung across its seaward side like a barrage. This leaves a flat wide strand, calm waters, and protection (usually!) from the worst of the elements. Whether launching a boat or going for a swim, fishing, or diving, the conditions are favourable. Add to that the stunning scenery, the clear air and waters, and its attraction, to visitors and fisherfolk alike, is obvious.

So it is clear that, between the site of the MacDonnell's Castle, overlooking the rocks by the Pollock Holes and NewFoundOut, and the West End, a fishing community of a few huts would have been established – probably some time in the early eighteenth century. There are reports too of cabins alongside the area we now know as the Carrigaholt road.

The idea of habitation at what we now know as Moore Bay was therefore already established by the 1790s when the great and the good of these islands took a fancy to the new fad of sea bathing.

There is an irony in the fact that, whilst the very remoteness of Kilkee made it attractive, it was the start of regular paddle steamer passages from Limerick to Kilrush in the 1820s that made the strand at Kilkee an accessible place for "taking the waters". From Kilrush, the journey to the town was made by horse and trap, and it was not long before Catty Fitzgerald had built Kilkee's first "hotel" – little more than an enlarged thatched cabin.

Many visitors were too grand to stay in such an establishment, and there began a trend, particularly among Limerick folk, for building seaside residences or "lodges" around the bay, where they could stay for the summer bathing season. Understandably, this encouraged more west Clare people to move into the area to provide services for the seasonal visitors, and its growth as a town was quite spectacular.

The Census figures tell us that, in 1821, there were 409 inhabitants in Kilkee but by 1841 there were 1590. The numbers increased further after the Famine, as people from the countryside moved into the town, bringing the population to 1904.

In the 1830s, three hotels were built – basically the major hotels which survived till the sixties, and in 1842 there were recorded over 230 houses, a post office, a school and two churches. Grattan St (then called Francis St) had over two dozen businesses.

It was a tale repeated around the coastlines of the British Isles throughout the first half of the 19th century. Sea Bathing became a huge attraction and various towns, devoted to enabling people to "take the waters", developed, to suit their own characteristics, their geographical positions, and the population patterns around them.

"Two Months at Kilkee" by Mary John Knott, published in 1836, tells us much about the town in these early days and about social attitudes and expectations.

An Gorta Mór hit west Clare hard, but in its aftermath the current appearance of the town began to take shape when the familiar sea wall was built as part of the Famine Relief scheme.

For Kilkee, growing as it was, folk from Limerick, rather than Clare, made up the majority of the visitors – because those paddle steamers from Limerick down the Shannon to Kilrush made it, for them, an easier journey than for folk from other parts of County Clare. A new "road" between Ennis and Kilrush: the "Mail line" had been constructed in the 1790s, and though it would have been far too basic to encourage families to travel on it, such a development must have contributed psychologically to the feeling that the west coast was not quite so remote as it had once seemed.

Given its location, transport developments were always crucial for the town, and the next boost to its importance as a resort came when the West Clare Railway, from Ennis to Miltown Malbay, was extended by the addition of the South Clare Railway to Kilrush and Kilkee in 1892.

The ability of the train to carry goods out to Kilkee had a huge impact on what the town could offer – but the ferrying of large groups of passengers started a transformation of the resort – from a bathing site for the wealthy and merchant classes, to a popular seaside place for a far wider section of society.

Kilkee was about to enter its heyday!

That is not to say that "summer holidays", as we know them now, were available to all at the turn of the century. Ordinary workers had profited from a handful of Bank Holidays from the early 1870s, and by the turn of the century, the skilled and managerial classes were starting to receive annual paid leave, something which was nowhere near universal for ordinary workers until the thirties or later.

Edwardian times were, however, the start of a recognition of the benefits of holidays – to workers, and to business owners - in terms of increased health and productivity. With the train and the Bank Holidays, more folk could reach Kilkee for "day trips", and as more visited, so its attractions became more widely popularised, and in the first decade of the century large numbers of visitors started to frequent Kilkee when their limited holiday time permitted.

Almost immediately it arrived in the town, the railway had started to eat into the passenger numbers carried by the steamers on the Shannon. However, as late as the end of the Great War, the ships still ran, and their demise was somewhat slowed by the availability of a joint steamer/railway ticket which would take you all the way to the seaside.

The Easter Rising, the War of Independence and the Civil War had a huge effect on the country as a whole, of course, but Kilkee was perhaps less involved than many places. Testimonies to the National Archives indicate that activity was at a low level in the town, as it relied so much on visitors during the summer season, and there is a suggestion that Crown Forces locally – such as the RIC, were restrained in their own activities because of this.

For all that, Kilkee lost Lt. John McSweeney, a member of the local Brigade's Active Service Unit, killed in action at Kildysart in August 1922, and respected Brigade Adjutant, Michael Fahy, who had died of wounds in March 1920.

Reports suggest that the West Clare Brigade IRA's Fifth Battalion, which covered the area, could muster no more than twenty men from the town, amongst whom were still familiar local names such as Marrinan and Talty. The Mid-Clare Brigade, which was active to the north of Kilkee, took part in more operations and thus attracted more reprisals.

Kilkee was, however, tangentially involved in two of the most notable actions in West Clare. On September 22nd 1920, the Mid-Clare Brigade launched a successful ambush at Rineen, just beyond Miltown Malbay. As a result of this, there were reprisals by the Black and Tans involving civilian deaths and the burning of premises in Miltown Malbay, Lahinch, Ennistymon, and Liscannor.

The same day, a former British officer, Alan Lendrum, who was Resident Magistrate at Kilkee, was ambushed at a level crossing near Doonbeg. The OC of the West Clare Brigade's Active Service Unit,

Liam Haugh, always maintained the attack was merely to obtain the RM's motor car, and that things got out of hand when he resisted the IRA instructions. Whatever the fact of the matter, the Crown Forces were enraged by his death, and by the Rineen incident, and their anger fuelled the reprisals. Two IRA volunteers from Doonbeg, Michael McNamara and Willie Shanahan, were killed while in custody later on in the year, as a result of these actions. There is a suggestion that it was only the intercession of Kilkee Parish Priest, Canon Glynn, that saved the town from a similar fiery fate to that of Lahinch and Ennistymon.

The local IRA also kept a close eye on the West Clare Railway, frequently raiding it to examine and "censor" mail for useful military intelligence.

It seems, at this remove, that the town's growing reputation as a seaside resort may have insulated it somewhat from the full horrors of the conflict, though houses were still raided, and many families from the country around Kilkee suffered harassment, or lost family members in military conflict.

What is true, however, is that this escape from reprisals on property contributed to the "Victorian feel" of the town later on, in the mid twentieth century, and helped maintain the town's appearance. It is not easy to imagine the brutality of war in such beautiful surroundings, but Kilkee's people made their contribution and bore the burden of all that is involved in military opposition to colonial rule. It is part of their history, and, as such, helped shape the town about which I am writing, remembering that my first visit in 1966 was only just over forty years since these events had taken place, and many townsfolk would still have a clear memory of all that had happened.

The new Free State grew slowly through the twenties and thirties, but the "Emergency" made life hard for Ireland. The isolationist policies pursued by De Valera's Government in the fifties led to massive emigration and, even today, a trip out through Cross, Kilballyowen, Moneen, Kilbaha and back through Carrigaholt reveals a ghostly trail of abandoned cottages and deserted fields, despite some recent regeneration and civic energy being brought to bear by the population.

However, Sean Lemass and T.K.Whittaker's new economic ideas, brought hope in the later fifties and into the sixties – and through all this time, however hard life was, trips to the seaside and, hence, the popularity of Kilkee, continued to flourish.

Limerick remained the mainstay of tourist support for the town, as adults who had holidayed in Kilkee as children returned to rent the same lodges they remembered from their youth. Business people from Limerick and Ennis and further afield, even to Dublin, bought houses in the town, to let out, and to stay in themselves. As transport improved and cars became more widespread – at least in the cities, it became common for families to spend a month or more at the seaside, and for the fathers/husbands to travel down for the weekends.

By the start of the sixties there was a kind of stability starting to grow in Ireland. The country as a whole, and perhaps the Shannon area in particular, received a huge boost from the visit of President Kennedy in June 1963, which in turn promoted tourism from abroad, especially from the USA and from the emigrant communities.

The Shannon stopover – forcing planes to and from the USA to call at the airport at Rineanna – was good for tourism in the Shannonside region – and the Kilkee hotels often benefited from bus loads of tourists, whose planes had been delayed overnight by weather or mechanical problems. There were established hotels in the area – like Dromoland Castle and the Old Ground at Ennis, but now newer businesses were appearing like the Clare Inn, the Limerick Inn and the West County Inn. Under the auspices of Bord Faílte, tourism was expanding in the west of the country, and Kilkee was a beneficiary.

In the early sixties, the idea of package holidays to Europe was having its small beginnings. I remember Tom Mannion Travel in Ennis and the Dublin-based Joe Walsh Tours who promoted trips to Spain and Italy. However, the fact was that it was still often necessary to start these tours by going via the UK to Europe, and this added time and expense for families who had already saved hard to be able to afford a holiday in the first place.

As a result, Irish seaside holidays were booming, and alongside Kilkee, towns such as Arklow, Ballybunnion, Tramore, Salthill, Lahinch and Bundoran were all doing well.

So this was the background to the Kilkee I reached in August of 1966. It was a well established family resort with visitors from all over Ireland, and, as we shall see, a fair number from overseas. It was busy, without being overwhelmingly so, as it was still at the end of quite a long road! Day trippers from Limerick and Ennis were common, but you could let your child wander over the road to the strand from the front garden of your Marine Parade lodge without being too worried about passing cars, and a walk around the bay would be almost guaranteed free from exhaust fumes or anti social behaviour.

It was, essentially, a family resort rather than a fashionable destination. Nowadays we would view the unsophisticated amusements and the tiny fairground as very simple and basic, but they fitted the town and they met the needs of folk who loved the place for that very simplicity. The golf course still only had nine holes, and the appearance of the town was little changed since the 1940s, apart from the addition of a hotel in the east end and a new church built at the start of the 60s.

This was partly what attracted generations of families to return to Kilkee year after year: the unchanging familiarity of the town and the welcome of its people. Holidaymakers who brought their families had often been brought to Kilkee by their own parents; they returned to the happy places of their youth, recognised the same faces each year, and built the tradition for their own children.

I was about to join them.

GETTING TO KNOW YOU

I had gone to bed on the day I arrived in Kilkee rather underwhelmed by the town. However, I had enjoyed the countryside between Shannon and Kilkee, and I was easily old enough to appreciate that West Clare weather would not be the same as that which I had experienced in continental Europe over the past five or six years' Summer holidays.

Nevertheless, the major impression I had gained on that first evening had been one of steady drizzle, raindrops on the dining room windows, and a seemingly endless expanse of mudflats around the bay.

When I got up and came down to breakfast on my first morning, it would be fair to say that the jury was still out on my new holiday experience.

However, pausing in the Lounge before I headed into breakfast, things seemed a lot brighter. People were heading in and out of the main entrance or coming out of the dining room; a few were sitting reading the papers or quietly chatting. There was a happy hum of activity.

Writing this fifty years later, I am aware suddenly, for the first time, of one of the contributory factors to the welcoming feel of the hotel. Laugh if you will – but it was the carpet!

The stairs and lounge were covered by a simple red carpet. By 1966 it was well worn. I don't mean it was ripped, stained, or threadbare, but rather that it had adjusted through its years of use to feel comfortable underfoot. It fitted the place perfectly and was unlike the more expensive, deeper piled carpets in high end hotels, or the cheap floor coverings found elsewhere. Subconsciously, what made you feel at home was what lay under your feet – a real welcome mat, you might say.

As I say, it may appear fanciful, but, through the years, I have come to realise that there was much more to Kilkee – and enjoying the town – than initially met the eye.

Come what may, I progressed to the dining room and received a warm welcome from the staff. As I sat down, my mother passed me the menu and so came another great discovery in my young lifetime: the Irish breakfast.

Grapefruit segments, porridge, bacon, egg, sausage, black pudding and tomato. Toast and honey to follow. All washed down by pots of tea. Now, I had long been a fan of cooked breakfasts – but this was a whole new experience. I suppose the biggest difference was that most of the ingredients would be fresh and locally sourced. These days such a claim would add to the appeal of an eating place, in 1966 it was simply the only option in Kilkee. To this day, every time I taste grapefruit segments, I'm taken back to the Hydro Hotel dining room.

The breakfast, allied to the friendliness of the staff, sent my spirits soaring, while, through the windows, I could see the tide had come in under high blue skies flecked with fluffy clouds – a holiday picture postcard of a scene. In retrospect, this was the moment when Ireland started to reclaim me, I suppose.

We left the dining room and walked out through the front door and surveyed the scene. Ahead of us the hotel garden lawns sloped down towards the road round the bay. There were colourful flower beds, a tennis court, croquet hoops, a putting green, and, along the side, in front of shrubs and bushes, hotel staff were putting out deckchairs. You could taste the salt in the air and the sun was bright enough to make you want to shield your eyes.

My mother said she would get her book and sit in the sun and I was free to go off and explore.

This was another big moment.

Of course, as a fourteen year old I had a fair amount of freedom at home, but the nature of our holidays in my childhood had meant that, once abroad, my mother and I had done everything together. It would hardly have been practicable for me to wander off alone in Madrid or Innsbruck. I have often thought that we went to Kilkee in 1966 because my mother felt I was of an age to enjoy "an Irish holiday", but it is just as likely that she recognised that our previous type of holidays would no longer work for a teenager and a widow.

Whatever the reasoning, I felt the surge of freedom that morning as I headed off from the Hydro to start my exploration of Kilkee.

In later years I would have thought nothing of heading down the lawn and leaping the low wall on to the road. On that first occasion, however, I took the road down to the front and slowly took in the view ahead of me.

Though I didn't know it, I was walking down Wellington Square West towards the sea front. It is perhaps a good moment to mention that for most of the years I spent visiting the town, I only knew the names of a handful of streets. I can't recall there being many street signs and it would only be if you saw an advertisement, perhaps, that you would work out the name of the street: "Williams of the Circular Rd" "Arcadia Cinema - O'Curry St". Most of the time we referred to places or roads with references to hotels or pubs: "Just down from the Strand" "The road by Murphy's café" "Outside Tom Kett's". It was only when I sat down to write this memoir that I realised the space in front of the Hydro was known as Wellington Square – and recently I was able to access the podcast of a fascinating talk to the Kilkee Civic Trust on the history of the street names of Kilkee from J.J. Hickie, courtesy of the fine Raidió Corca Baiscinn. I suppose the cavalier attitude to street names formed part of the laid back charm of the place – especially to those of us who travelled from outside the country to stay there.

My memory of that first morning in the town remains crystal clear, however.

As I crossed the road to the wall, I remember the light and heat reflected up from the concreted pavement, it surface pricked with holes in the style of the times, to make it less slippery when wet.

The wall was all greys and greens, topped with regularly spaced upright stone slabs, which protruded from the surface, almost dividing it into seating spaces. As I leaned on the top of the wall and looked over to the strand I was met with what is probably my most resonant connection to Kilkee, even to this day: the sharp and tangy scent of drying seaweed wafting up from the rocks below.

Some folk found it too strong or even unpleasant, but for me, especially when it was mixed with the smoke of burning turf – as it was frequently in those days, it was sign to my brain that I had arrived in Kilkee.

I've found faint echoes of that seaweed smell on coasts all over the world, but it is never quite the same, and I know lots of other folk associate it with Kilkee, and Kilkee alone.

So, from that first morning my senses were fully assaulted by Kilkee – the smell of the seaweed, the sound of the waves and sea birds and swimmers, the salt on my lips, the feel of the stone on my skin and, before me, that glorious view of the bay.

On the face of things, Moore Bay is the unique selling point of Kilkee, the town having been gifted an almost magical setting – but I also think it is the combination of elements which make the place so special.

From the wall at the West End, where I was on that first morning, and which I still think is the best viewpoint in the town, there is the smooth strand, the colours of the grass behind the sand and the lodges round the strandline. George's Head rises in the distance, the pier points out into the bay, where there may be a couple of boats nodding at anchor and, on that first morning, even the architectural nightmare of the Atlantic Hotel in the East End seemed to be put in its place by the natural surroundings. Behind the town, hills roll gently away, and at all points round the bay, the black and brown rocks are given white and cream lace tapestry covers by the relentless tide – which has shaped the landscape for thousands of years.

Even the disturbed waters around the Duggerna Reef across the entrance to the bay – which can boil up a range of colours, from pure white to startling turquoise – seem to emphasise the difference between the unpredictable ocean and the more usually peaceful inner waters of the bay

Standing at the wall that morning in early August of 1966, I would have taken all of this in subconsciously, but it is fair to say that familiarity adds detail and context to the views we see.

More immediately, it was my surroundings which took my eye. As I mentioned, the pavement and wall reflected up a very pleasant warmth, even though it was not yet lunchtime. The influence of the Gulf Stream and the South Atlantic drift can be seen all along the south western coasts of Ireland, but I had not really been prepared for the mildness of the air in west Clare, even on occasions when the weather was less than summer like.

The wall was high at this point, with a drop of around 30 feet to the sand. I did not yet understand the meaning of the white oblongs for racquets, on the wall just below me, but there were low, half covered rocks jutting out of the sand below at the bottom of the wall, with seaweed draped across them.

To my left was a bigger outcrop of rock with a white painted wall to contain it, and a shelter, in which, presumably, swimmers could change. There were already a few families scattered around this area, towels on the rocky ledges, children paddling in the shallow water below at the edge of the strand, adults chatting, reading, or lying back in the sun.

I breathed deeply and felt myself relax.

I was aware that folk were walking behind me in both directions, with that easy walk which comes from being on holiday. There seemed to be a mixture of ages from the very young with their parents, to teenagers and older folk – all with their own pace, their own chatter, and their own thoughts.

I decided to head further west. The road curved round out of sight and I was interested to see what lay round the corner.

However, as is usually the case in Kilkee, I was waylaid by my surroundings.

First, on my left I became aware of a large building quite unlike the low squat buildings around it. It looked more like a barracks building than anything else – an appearance promoted by a decorative badge on its façade. People were playing croquet on its front lawns, towels were laid out to dry. Something else for me to wonder about. As I headed along the sea wall, I was on a learning curve!

Then, as I almost reached the turn in the road, I saw that the sea was a little wilder here, the rocks more extensive and as high as the road in places. A gap in the wall proved irresistible and I headed through on to the rocks.

I had always lived near the sea, and loved it. This chance to explore the pools, watch the surge of the tide, examine the rocks, and just relax with the stunning views, was perfect for me. With the exception of reading, and, sometimes, music, I know of few other pastimes which can be so completely absorbing and satisfying, and just plain captivating, as investigating rocks and their sea pools, their marine life and their evidence of millions of years of geological history. It is the privilege of the only child to be able to devote endless time to such interests; I was comfortable in my own company, and delighted to be able to enjoy it against such a perfect and engaging backdrop.

Darting fish, limpets clinging on for dear life, seaweed fronds that waved at you in the gently moving water and then shied away when you tried to touch them, and little movements under pebbles that were indistinct and impossible to identify. Scuttling crabs, shells that were deep blue, cream, brown, white and black, and diamonds of light that hurt your eyes as the pools captured the shine of the sun and cast it back in your face.

Oh that was a magical first experience of Edmond Point outside of Sykes's House. Like so many other parts of Kilkee, and so many other experiences, it was simply special.

When I checked my watch eventually, I was amazed to find it was already lunchtime. Back on the road, I looked west and saw a high hill rising in the distance, more rocks, sea and cliffs, people moving sideways like crabs, across the exposed parts of the reef. It all looked rather wonderful, but, it amuses me to think now, I was unsure of my way about – I feared "getting lost", so I headed back to the Hydro, buzzing with excitement and filled with plans for further exploration.

Of course, on that August morning, I thought I had made a discovery; I thought I was the only one who had thrilled to discover Kilkee. It was a feeling reinforced when I returned to school and raved about the place. Most of my friends, even those from Irish families, knew nothing about Ireland other than their homeplace and maybe Dublin. To them, as much as to me, Kilkee was a new discovery, though I was never entirely sure that they understood my raptures about it.

But, the years went by, and, as you would expect, I would discover there were thousands of people all over the world for whom the name "Kilkee" evokes happiness, memories, and perfection.

The beauty of Kilkee is that it is not a solo preoccupation, it's a love affair shared with many.

It is, in large measure, for those folk that I am writing this memoir.

34

THE HYDRO

When I decided to compose this memoir, I wondered if I should attempt to write it chronologically. Certainly, starting with my first visit to the town makes some kind of sense.

However, I visited Kilkee every Summer between 1966 and 1975, and between 1970 and 1985 I paid at least one visit to the town outside of the Summer season, often staying there on two or more occasions during the year.

Many of the people I met in Kilkee were either residents, or visitors who returned year by year, so I am afraid at this distance it is not always possible to pinpoint in which year which event happened. Furthermore, I am concerned with capturing the flavour of holidays in Kilkee in years gone by and I am not sure that exact dates would add anything to that concept.

That being the case, I will divide my memories up into different areas and write about them with limited reference to the years involved.

Given I was a holidaymaker, it seems reasonable to start by focusing on the hotels in which I stayed.

Over the years, I have reckoned I stayed in seven establishments in the town – most of them on more than one occasion. They would be the Hydro, the Victoria, the Marine, the Strand, the Stella Maris, the

Esplanade and the Ocean Cove, though the last was long after the sixties. I also spent a couple of nights in a shed in the garden behind Peggy O'Halloran's shop in the Circular Rd and, the odd time, slept in the shelter up near the Golf Club if we had been out all night!

My memories are, of course, subjective and personal, but, I hope, as accurate a recollection as I can capture, given the passage of fifty years.

I debated long and hard whether or not I should name people in this memoir, especially the many whom I have not met or been in touch with for decades. However, I have nothing less than positive to say about any of them, and, in my memory at least, the people – whether visitors or residents – were part of the attraction of my Kilkee holidays. I hope nobody will be displeased should they spot their name in these pages, and I send my apologies to any whom I may have inadvertently misrepresented in any way.

My first focus must be on the Hydro Hotel. It was my original "home from home" in the town, and, if I am honest, has always remained the dearest to me as representing all that was good about Kilkee holidays. Of course, it benefited, like a poet or politician who dies young, from disappearing from the scene relatively quickly and therefore avoiding any kind of decline or change of atmosphere, as the years passed.

The Hydro Hotel – or Moores, or Old Moores as it had been variously known, was one of the town's original hotels, dating back, I suppose, in one form or other to the 1830s, though changing to suit the fashions as the decades rolled by.

Though it has now been converted into holiday apartments, the basic appearance – the white maritime outline, faintly art deco, with the tower like a mast at one end – was similar in 1966. At the other end, the bottom of the hill, was the Ballroom, of which more later, and the window frames and doors, standing out against the white painted stonework, were a deep red – echoed by the lettering for "Hydro" running down the tower, and "Ballroom" written above the dancehall.

It stood out to visitors– partly due to design and paintwork, but also because of its pre-eminent position in the West End, emphasised by the lawns sloping down in front of the long low building.

Its name said something about its past and its pretensions. "Hydropathic" establishments, from Victorian times onwards, had advertised themselves as being places not just for holidays and recreation, but to promote health, and this was particularly true of the seaside.

Though the Thalassotherapy Centre has been re-established in Kilkee for decades now, the use of the sea and its products to promote health and wellbeing is ancient, and was certainly an original selling point when the craze for bathing started to flourish in the late eighteenth century. However, it hardly featured in the sixties at all, but the Hydro would have heavily promoted itself as supporting health and wellness in its early days.

The definition of "Hydro" moderated over the years, till it came to reflect a hotel where there were many activities and pastimes available. When I first arrived in Kilkee, the Hydro provided tennis, table tennis, putting and croquet, as well as dancing, and the flower beds and plant boxes along the front of the hotel, so carefully tended by Timmy McInerney, added. a feeling of relaxation and calm.

So, even in its name, the Hydro seemed to be offering more than just a hotel experience.

As I have hinted, there was a homeliness about the place which made its guests feel very comfortable and at ease. An hotel inspector may have described the building as rather "tired" but the fact remained that it attracted people from all walks of life who tended to return year by year. That seems to suggest it was doing something right, for a time, at any rate.

Going in the front entrance, which was towards the top of the slope, under the tower, as I've mentioned, you would see the tiny reception desk straight ahead – with barely room for one clerk and two guests to stand at it. To the left was the long lounge. It was divided into two levels by three steps half way along its length, which made it cosy and comfortable for groups of people to sit round tables and chat or read, or have a drink.

When I first visited, there was a tiny bar to the right of the entrance and beyond that the dining room. Within a couple of years, the small bar was converted into a "steak house' for the dining of non-residents, and a new and larger bar was built along the front of the hotel, linking to the Ballroom. This, I suspect, reflected the realisation that bar profits and the attraction of non-residents, were a sure way to boost profitability. Crucially, I think, the new bar and the residents' lounge remained separate, which probably helped both to flourish.

Of course, on my first visit, I had no idea of the hotel's history. Had you told me Alfred, Lord Tennyson had stayed there, I probably would have disbelieved you. I didn't really have a feel either for the role it played in the resort as a social centre, though I quickly picked up that, amongst the guests, there was a very pleasing and comfortable mix of backgrounds.

Probably my initial impression was of the friendly and relaxed nature of the place and, in particular, the staff – who were mostly local – from the town or west Clare, and, in those days, all Irish.
I suppose having memory of so many staff names from those days reveals how welcoming they were to this young lad with a strange accent from across the sea.

At various times in the dining room we shared laughs with Cyril Costello, who would tease us about the egg flips at Fanny O'Dea's, Rita, Frances Ryan from Kilmihil, Martina Scanlon from Carrigaholt, Ann Devitt, Elizabeth Jennings, Breige Keightley, Ann Marie and Josephine Frawley, Ann Foran, Doonbeg's Mary McGrath, and many others.

Among the porters were Senan, Brendan, Eugene Costello, Olly Frawley, Michael McGrath, and a Clohessy or two. I had some great chats with P.J. Foran when he was night porter, and, of course, as many staff returned year by year, looking forward to meeting up with them again was part of the draw of each August Summer holiday.

I don't know how many of these folk look back on their times in the Hydro favourably – or if they even look back at all. Such are my happy memories of the hotel that these names inhabit my recollections, forever eighteen or nineteen, dressed in the blue waitresses' uniforms or porters' white jackets, always ready for a laugh or a chat.

Some became friends, whom we saw outside of hotel working hours. I remember once helping to smuggle the chef, Ron May, from Limerick, out of a tiny window in the staff quarters, for some middle of the night adventure, and so many happy times with Pauline Carberry, and Margaret Flanagan from Laois, who worked in housekeeping, and Noreen Guiney from Kilballyowen who also worked in the dining room. I once bumped into another chef, Mikey Keane, on the Liverpool ferry.

Fifty years later, of course, these are just names to be remembered, companions for a few weeks each summer, before our lives took off into the adult world and paths never crossed again. But, when we think of holidays, we think of people as well as places, and the Hydro staff, as much as anyone, contributed to my happy times in the town.

For some reason which I never fully understood, my mother had a talent for getting on with staff – she was friendly and open with them and, I guess, offered some relief from more formal or demanding guests.

She would chat with the reception staff: Meta, Hynes, Gaby and Anna – who eventually married our taxi driver P.J. King – and made a particular friendship with the hotel manageress, Barbara Weldon.

It was only recently I came across a picture in the Clare Libraries Collection of "Hydro Hotel Staff". By the styles worn, it may have been late forties, early fifties – and there was a younger version of Barbara, underlining her commitment to the Hydro as manager through the years.

Anyone who was in Kilkee in those days will remember her well. To me as a fourteen year old, she was quite formidable in a school teachery sort of way. She certainly kept a firm grip on her staff, but I suspect there was a twinkle behind the eye sometimes, which I was not clever enough to spot. If you never knew Barbara, I think I could best describe her as appearing as you would expect Paul Brady's mother to be, greying red hair in a severe bun, and gold rimmed glasses. I would love to have known more about her because I suspect she would have had an interesting history.

I did get to know her brother Gus and his family who were often staying at the hotel at the same time as we were. Gus Weldon was a lovely, kind, and amusing man, who had some fame in his own right as the owner of the Pearl Bar in Dublin's Fleet St – a noted hangout for journalists, writers, and Dublin characters at the time.

The story was told by Gus of how Brendan Behan and Patrick Kavanagh fell out one day in the bar, and the argument progressed till the point where the bold Brendan was hanging Kavanagh out of the first floor window by his heels. His friends pulled Paddy in, and he fled into the street to escape the wrath of Behan, finally taking refuge in a confessional box in St Andrew's Church.

Given that the Pearl was also an R&R site for journalists from the Irish Times building opposite, I expect Gus found his holidays at his sister's hotel an oasis of peace after the shenanigans in Fleet St.

He was a very sociable man and we became friendly with his family – daughter, Bernadette and sons Peter and Paul. Peter and I maintained a friendship for many years, and the family were once hospitable hosts when we stayed a night as students in their home in Ballsbridge.

This was a friendship which echoed many we made in Kilkee, and especially at the Hydro. It was many years later when I realised that Barbara Weldon had so much history with the Hydro, and that Gus was so relatively well known on the Dublin scene. I think now how amazing it would have been to ask him about Behan and Kavanagh and the rest of them – but that would have made the relationship between our families something different, and so I am glad for my ignorance. A lot of it was caused by my youth – and more possibly, by coming from another country and, in those pre-internet days, knowing little about Ireland.

Patrick Kavanagh, and my ignorance, again feature in another friendship we were to make in those early Hydro years.

I have mentioned that my mother would often spend her days reading and sunbathing on a deckchair in the Hydro gardens. Apart from the relaxation, it was a good chance to make friends amongst the guests and she made a number of lasting friendships in that way.

Naturally, when I spent any time in the garden, (or called in for fresh supplies of cash!), I would be introduced to her new friends.

One such was a striking woman, with ash blonde hair, frequently wearing large sunglasses. My mother introduced her as "Hilda" and it turned out their friendship had been cemented by the fact that she had recently been widowed and was interested to hear my mother's experiences, as someone who had similarly lost her husband at a relatively young age.

It transpired that the woman's husband had been a politician, though initially we were aware of neither his identity nor his importance.

The following year we noticed election posters as we passed by Limerick, with her photo and a request to "Vote O'Malley, Hilda".

She had lost that election – in a bitter battle with her husband's nephew, Dessie O'Malley, and, gradually, her story – and that of the charismatic Donogh, her late husband, was revealed to us.

That second year, her children were with her, and we got to know them as well. Suzanne, the eldest, was generally away doing her own thing – though she did introduce me to the great Limerick band, Granny's Intentions. Her brother, Daragh, was a couple of years younger than me, and spent rather more time with the gang of youngsters who stayed at the Hydro. I thought I could sense the sadness of the loss of his dad about him, and he was rather mercurial, but generally good company.

One benefit of Daragh's friendship was that he could gain access to a lodge the family owned in Geraldine Place, down the side of the hotel. It looked like it had not been used by the family for some time, but it was perfect for our group. We would scatter ourselves round the darkened front room late at night, candles lit as befitted the hippy times we were living in, and listen to Tim Hardin's songs on Peter Weldon's battery powered record player. As I write that I can see it is a description of a distant time, far removed from mobiles and Beats headphones, but the memory of those nights has lingered a lifetime as a reminder of what it is to be young – at least in those days.

Without knowing anything more about Hilda at the time, I found her extremely engaging. She was very attractive in a way which went beyond her looks. This was only three or four years after Dallas, and I'm sure I wasn't the only one to see parallels between Hilda and that other widow, Jackie Kennedy. She had that rare ability, which not all adults achieve, to treat teenagers as equals. I can picture the scene even now quite clearly.

I would sit on the grass nearby and she would close her book, push her sunglasses up and say – in that distinctive deep voice: "Hallo, John – what have you been up to?" – and it always seemed like she was interested in the answer. She would talk to me of books, education, my ambitions – real "grown up" conversations – in such a way that I was never tongue tied or nervous in her company.

Perhaps if I had known then what I was to find out years later I may have been less calm in my dealings with her.

"Raglan Road" had long been one of my favourite poems and songs before I discovered that Patrick Kavanagh had written it about Hilda. Even meeting her all those years later, it was easy to see why he had "loved too much". By all accounts, when a medical student, at the time the poet fell for her, she had been considered one of the most beautiful women in Dublin, and even had a screen test in Hollywood.

I also learned of the charm and energy of her late husband – one of Fianna Fail's "men in mohair suits" and he became rather a hero of mine for his inspired introduction of free secondary education across the country – the presager of later economic and academic success for Ireland. I often wondered too what would have become of his career, had he not died so young. The later advancement of his peers: Blaney, Lenihan, Boland and Haughey, provided some of the most interesting moments in later 20th century Irish politics. You would have to believe that "Dunnick", as he was known, would not have been far away from either innovation or controversy.

I kept in touch with Hilda for many years, writing the annual Christmas card to the family home in Roses Avenue, off Limerick's North Circular Rd. I know that, as a committed medic, she did much good work with the vulnerable in Limerick and Ennis. When I later fell in love with Dingle and Corca Dhuibhne, it didn't surprise me to hear that Hilda had been a Moriarty from that part of the world. There was something of that about her – though I would not have recognised it at the time. I am just glad that knowing her was one of the many gifts given to me by the Hydro.

Daragh – or at least news of him – continued to flit in and out of my life.

On the day before my 20th birthday I met Richard Harris in Southport, Lancashire, where my mother still lived and where he would be giving a concert the following night. We chatted about Kilkee – and Daragh - and how he had succeeded at LAMDA. Next day would turn out to be Derry's Bloody Sunday – which quite overshadows the memory, the concert, and my birthday.

Through the years, in films and television, Daragh's familiar appearance would loom, bringing back memories of Geraldine Place, until, eventually, he became world famous as "Sergeant Harper" alongside Sean Bean in the blockbuster series "Sharpe". It was good to link up with him again a few years ago through the facility of Facebook, and even better to share the odd memory of those Kilkee days.

Hilda O'Malley wasn't the only unexpected political encounter I had in the Hydro over the years. In the 1960s, Irish politics was still very much in the shadow of the Civil War: Fianna Fail against the treaty, Fine Gael in favour, meaning it was, to an extent, tribal, rather than policy based. The tendency for family members to "inherit" Dail seats added to this atmosphere. Furthermore, RTE – the national television service - was less than a decade old – and still coming to terms with how best to channel political debate.

The result was that old style political campaigning was still very much in vogue – and this led to client politics – what the Americans would refer to as "pork belly", and it was important for politicians to be "seen around" – whether at local funerals, the mart, or, so it seemed, in holiday spots.

Even as a sixteen year old, I had already been in the company of politicians in the Hydro Bar – and had drinks bought for me – in a kind of 'drinks on the house" scatter gun approach – which included all in the bar – voters or otherwise.

Paddy Hillery, who later became President, was a local man – from Miltown Malbay, and coincidentally, had been in the same medical course as Hilda Moriarty, as she then was, at University. He was more relaxed company than the other heavyweight with whom we spent a few hours – Brian Lenihan, whose larger than life personality would see him go far, and then fall, on the national scene. I never met Charles Haughey in Kilkee, though he was reputed to "solve major issues" whilst walking on George's Head. His enemies might have said it would be a brave opponent who would walk on the high cliffs with him! Dessie O'Malley, future Progressive Democrat's founder, nephew of Donogh, and Hilda's vanquisher in the Limerick East election, had a house on the cliff in the east end of the town, though I never saw him around.

These were just further examples of Kilkee's propensity to surprise you with those you met and the events which took place – the brief earlier visit of Che Guevara to the town, now celebrated annually in Che Do Bheatha, would be another example.

Limerick's Richard Harris, or "Dickie" as he was known locally, was perhaps the other most famous visiting celebrity – his links to the town, and to the racquet alleys, going back to his childhood.

His brother, Dermot, stayed at the Hydro when we were there, once including Richard's children, Damian, Jared and Jamie in the party. You would not have known of the connection; Dermot spent a lot of time nursing a hangover behind dark glasses, and his wife, Cassie was a bundle of energy with the children. She was a lovely person, later the wife of Pierce Brosnan, and sadly died young. "Celebrity" was a different experience in those days – or maybe that was just at the Hydro.

As I've said, I was scarcely aware that many of these folk I was meeting had a resonance beyond the hotel, and the major advantage of Hydro holidays for me was that, as an only child, I had access to a gang of friends with whom to explore the town and get up to teenage mischief.

Again, one of the further attractions was that these folk were from a variety of backgrounds – none of which impacted at all on our activities or friendships.

There was the Ryder family from Dublin, with their children Bernadette and James – who was the first Bohs supporter I ever met! The James's from London's Surrey stockbroker belt, with their daughters, Frances and Gaye, were regular guests. Frances caused great confusion by announcing they had stopped for lunch in "Car Hire" – only her revelation that it was in Tipperary bringing the realisation that she was referring to Cahir.

We became friendly with the Drislanes who also lived in Surrey. Anita and her sister Gay were part of the "Hydro Gang" and her dad, a GP, was a great source of fun and had come originally from Shanagolden across the Shannon.

Another pal was Tony Wilson, whose family ran a pub in North Belfast, and who had been coming to Kilkee for years, and the Youngs, Frank and Nick, came from Liverpool – their father was an Anglican Canon at a church in the city centre. Mary and Frank Dillon, from Coleraine, the Corboys from Clara in Offaly, David O'Keefe, from Ennis, Margaret Bennett – a piper with Agnes O'Connell's London Irish Girl Pipers – the friendships were many,

and our exchange of letters throughout the year stoked up our anticipation of the annual August meetings.
There were other folk who were part of the "Hydro Family" but who tended to do their own thing during the day, returning to the hotel in the evening.

As I will write later, I fell in love with showband dances at the Hydro Ballroom – for lots of reasons, so, when the BBC broadcast RTE's documentary on Dickie Rock and the Miami just before my second visit to Kilkee, I was a very interested observer. Predictably, given it was the sixties, the angle of the film was that the Miami were "Ireland's Beatles" –and, certainly, the scenes shown from their appearances backed up the frenzy that they created across the land at the time.

We were discussing this film in the lounge a few weeks later with a family called the Carney's, from Dublin.

Their dad, Des, suddenly said to us: "Would you like to see the Miami?"

It turned out that the band were playing in Kilkee that night – in a marquee specially set up in the field at the entry to town which is now occupied by the Gaelic grounds. Marquee dances, especially as part of festivals, were very common in those days – even in towns with established ballrooms.

Des Carney was Dickie Rock's GP and he said he could get us in despite the gig being sold out.

It was one of those accidental moments in life which resonate for decades. If ever a scene deserved the description "the joint was rocking", this would have been it.

The east end of the town was gridlocked with cars parked anywhere, anyhow. Light and noise was pulsing out from the huge tent which was surrounded by folk – young and not so young – trying to "sneak a look" through the flapping canvas.

None of this was a problem for Des who got us in with a wink and a nod. We were met by a wave of noise, light and heat – but mostly by a mass of humanity and a heady mix of perfume, cigarette smoke, alcohol fumes and sweat.

Dickie was leading the band in a cover of Anita Harris's current hit "Just Loving You" –so the marquee was a gently but powerfully moving mass of slow dancing couples. He spotted Des and waved to us all from the stage. We tried to make our way to the side of the floor.

"Your next dance, please!" was followed quickly by the opening brass of the band's current number one hit: "Baby, I'm your man."

At this stage, I had not started going to rock concerts at home: that would come a few months later in November 1967. I had seen the bands at the Hydro the previous year – but I was completely unprepared for the power of this moment and an eight man band driving their way through a hit single. It was like a wall of sound – not an original description, but the only one that really fits. As everybody started dancing, the dance floor at our side of the marquee started to rise and fall in time to the beat. There was that rare one-ness between performers and audience when all was focused on the music and the rhythm. It wasn't the greatest song ever written, but the impact of sound, time, and place, left an indelible impression on me. It was, quite simply an unforgettable experience, and though I have since seen the Stones, the Who, Fleetwood Mac, McCartney, Springsteen, Dire Straits and the rest, I'm not sure anything in the world of music has left me quite so stunned as that one moment – when a band on top of its form played for a holiday making crowd in the heat of a field marquee in Kilkee, County Clare.

Though the personnel had changed, you can imagine the sadness I felt six years later when the Miami made rather more tragic headlines after the massacre outside of Banbridge during the Troubles.

The Carneys brought their family with them, and mostly I remember daughters Maria and Leonora. Maria, who would have been three or four years older than me, was a tall red head with stunning looks, and, with my Christian Brothers' education and shy, only child, status, she seemed to me to be operating on another planet, with her confidence and self possession.

But if Maria silenced me when she passed, I'm sure there were times when Leonora's presence left me slack jawed. She was only a year or so older than me, but, even in mundane conversation with her I became tongue tied. Without a doubt she was beautiful, but her effect was more due to an insouciant style. She dressed simply and, to my sheltered eyes anyway, seemed totally unaware of how impressive she was. Friendly and relaxed, she was fitted to the era, with long tumbling hair and a kind of energy about her.

She was also to be, unconsciously and without intention, the source of one of my lifelong inabilities.

Leonora had a boyfriend working in Dublin. He used to come down each weekend to see her. Because she was attractive, naturally he had a little red open topped sports car. To me, as an innocent fifteen year old, that was one of the rules of the universe: boys with sports cars got attractive girlfriends.

Anyway, he was a pleasant lad, though, perhaps understandably, we didn't see a lot of the couple during the weekends he was down. Each Sunday evening he would leave to drive back to Dublin and one Sunday I happened to be in front of the hotel when he was leaving.

Now, I have to emphasise again, there was no "attitude" in this couple, no showing off, or display of superiority. To me they were glamour personified, but they never acted as if they thought that themselves.

This particular day he was later than usual in leaving and clearly in a rush. He ran out of the hotel, gave Leonora a quick kiss, flung all his gear into the back of the car, and drove off, literally, into the sunset.

There is a scene in David Lean's "Ryan's Daughter" – of which more later – when hero Tim O'Leary, the Rebel Leader, thanks local girl, Moureen Cassidy, for gathering arms off the beach for him. He gives her a peck on the cheek and turns away. Moureen stands there motionless in the tumult of the storm, stars in her eyes, hair wild in the wind, rain running down her face, lost in her dream at what has just happened.

I have often thought I must have been something like that the night that the boyfriend drove off. I remember thinking, as you do at that age: "God, I'd love to do that one day!"

Sadly, the sports car never materialised – but I did achieve, and have maintained, that cavalier approach to packing – whether travelling by car, train, boat or plane, my approach is generally: chuck it all in and hope for the best.

This causes understandable distress amongst my loved ones. But my inevitable response is always: "Blame the Hydro and Leonora's boyfriend!."

By all accounts, and in achievement far beyond her boyfriend's influence on my packing, I believe Leonora has become a much respected concert pianist and music teacher. I don't doubt she does both with the same self possession and grace which so impressed the teenage me!

Another Dublin family who were often in the Hydro when we were there were the Linders, and, though at the time they were chiefly famous as "Linders of Smithfield", the garage owners, they had a certain amount of glamour about them. The children, Joe and Kay, both had dark good looks and a lot of confidence, and though ages in general with the rest of the young ones, never really operated as part of our group. Kay was one of the most beautiful girls I had ever met and possessed a level of sophistication which I am not sure I have ever attained, even yet!

The brother and sister were highly competitive, and I remember one day they challenged each other to a swim across the bay. When I see the organisation and crowds which attend the "big bay" and "small bay" swims these days, it's hard to credit their race in the sixties.

Basically, half of us went to the pier and the rest over to the bathing shelter at the west end. To the best of my recollection there were no adults, no lifesavers, no safety boats – just Kay and Joe equally determined to win the race. To be fair, I think they were both strong swimmers, but it was certainly the action of a couple of very motivated, proud, and determined people.

They jumped in off the pier and we all watched as they battled the waves cross to the far side. I may be mistaken, but my memory is that Kay won and Joe was less than pleased. Apologies if I have that wrong!

I don't know what happened to Kay – but I am sure she continued to dazzle. Joe expanded the family business into property development and has been a major player in various ways around the Dublin scene, but, to me, they are always that brother and sister bringing a spot of glamour to the Hydro and swimming the bay in sibling rivalry!

One more Hydro event and one more memorable character remain to be described.

I have mentioned my upbringing in Scotland and England, and the fact that, while my family's Irish origins were never hidden, neither were they exactly promoted. We listened to the RTE News each day at 1.30 – and were great fans of Frankie Byrne's lunchtime radio problem page as well. However, we were not part of an Irish emigrant community in any sense. My mother had been a member of the Gaelic League, and attended the Irish Centre in Liverpool, but there were no Irish dance, music or language lessons for me, so I didn't arrive in Kilkee with a strong sense of my heritage.

This meant that the idea of a "session" – as in a gathering where everybody took their turn to sing a song or recite a piece – was quite foreign to me.

However, thanks to the Hydro, I was about to become very familiar with the idea.

Nowadays, tourist towns abound with "craic agus ceol" pub signs, and organised sessions, on a nightly basis, at the height of the season, are taken for granted – but it should be remembered that the traditional music revival in Ireland was only in its slow beginnings when I first came to Kilkee. Johnny McEvoy with "The Boston Burglar", Danny Doyle with "Whiskey on a Sunday", and Dermot O'Brien with "The Merry Ploughboy" were about the height of it, though the songs of the Dubliners and the Clancy Brothers were also becoming popular.

Christy Moore has said that his impetus to join the traditional music scene full time came with the bankers' strike in 1966, but it was not until 69 and 72 that his first two albums were released, and 73 when we heard the first Planxty release.

So in the mid sixties, unless you were in a particular hot bed of traditional music, you would have been unlikely to find regular sessions in most pubs. The "seisún" only grew in popularity and frequency towards the end of the decade. Indeed, I remember going to a bar in Cappagh, on the Shannon shore, out beyond Kilrush, where we must have seen one of the earliest Wolfe Tones performances.

For all that, the tradition of "doing a turn" remained strong – and, at this, the Hydro Residents' Lounge excelled.

Though, in later years, the hotel sometimes employed a pianist or MC to get things moving, in my earliest visits it was a completely informal affair, and its impact on me, its novelty, and its resonance, were perhaps one of my major reason for wanting to write this memoir and record what happened on those August nights in the Hydro.

Its informality was one of the attractions: you would never know if there would be a session that night or not. It depended on which of the 'prime movers' happened to be in the lounge, whether folk lingered after midnight, or went elsewhere, or to bed, early in the evening. One night a week there was no dance in the Ballroom and this could affect which of the younger group were around the hotel. Occasionally word got round of something happening elsewhere – in the Strand, the Westcliff, Ketts, at Lynch's in Doonaha, or at Taylor's of Moyasta – and there would be an exit of people looking for entertainment. Mostly, however, it happened in the Hydro lounge and started quite naturally as people realised someone had started to sing, or perhaps somebody shouted: "Quiet please – for the singer."

The music scene being in such a time of change – and the residents in the lounge being all ages from 80 to 12 years old, another charming element of the entertainment was the unpredictability of each turn. You could have a McCormack tenor version of "Roses of Picardy" or "The Kerry Dances", followed by The Dubliners' "Dirty Old Town" and a version of "The Wearing of the Green". "Step it out, Mary" might be followed by "Yesterday" or "Anyone who had a heart", while the night could finish with "The West's Awake", "The Patriot Game" and "Good night, Irene. You would hear songs from the musicals: "Oh what a beautiful morning!", "I feel pretty", "Consider yourself at home" or "There is nothing like a dame". Running through most evenings were the familiar ballads which always retained their popularity: "The Wild Rover", "Kelly the Boy from Killane", "Sliabh na mBan,", "Whiskey in the Jar", and "Boolavogue".

In reality, the content and style was only limited by the variety of folk who were in the hotel on any given night. Most folk had a party piece, and it was not unusual to hear a recitation of "Dangerous Dan McGrew" or a similar monologue, as well as comedy songs, and, occasionally, long drawn out shaggy dog stories. I learned a lot about many different types of music on those long Hydro nights – and it seemed to be a time when people were content to appreciate any type of music, rather than categorising styles and closing their ears to "classical" or "pop" or "Irish" or any music they thought they wouldn't like. It also brought a unity to the hotel guests, as folk you saw through the day would be revealed as having a good musical voice, or a love of ballads, or the ability to tell a funny tale effectively.

Easily the most memorable of the lounge resident performers was a District Justice from the bench in Dundalk: Dermott Dunleavy.

"The Judge", as we called him, was a small, dapper man: I can see him now, dressed in a sharp houndstooth check sports jacket, distinguished greying hair swept back, and a smiling face that inescapably reminded you of "Mr Punch". It always seemed as if he needed to be persuaded to start singing, but, once he was in full flow, there was no stopping him, and he was obviously a born entertainer.

His speciality was the songs of Percy French; he was my introduction to the work of the Roscommon born entertainer, and, for me, Dermott's interpretation of the songs is always the one I hear in my head.

He didn't just sing the songs, he performed them, and his little bits of "business" – the tip of the head, the raising of a hand, the pause for a smile, lent the songs great power and wit.

He had a broad repertoire: "Phil the Fluther's Ball", "Come back Paddy Reilly", "The Mountains of Mourne", "McBreen's Heifer", Slattery's Mounted Fut", "Whistlin' Phil McHugh" were all favourites. However, his two highlights, and the songs which folk in the lounge were forever requesting, were "Drumcolliher" and "Are ye Right there, Michael?".

His timing on both was exquisite. He would pause quite markedly before the chorus of the first song and then invite us all to join in – a tactic he also used in "Come Back, Paddy Reilly" – and I can see and hear him in my mind's eye even now as he led the chorus:

"I suppose ye've not been to Drumcolliher?
Ye haven't? Well now I declare……."

There's something affecting about a large group of folk joining in with a softly sung chorus: it feels reflective, thoughtful and bonding – and it never failed to have this effect at the Hydro. I suppose a couple of pints of Smithwicks and a few Jameson Crested 10s also helped the midnight mood!

The other, more boisterous, facet to the emotional effect was that garnered by what is perhaps French's most famous song: "Are ye right there, Michael?"

This account of an attempt to reach Kilkee by the West Clare Railway was lent additional power by the fact that French had been headed for a concert in Moore's Hall – the Hydro Ballroom, only yards from where we were sitting, when he was given cause to write a song about his frustrations. At the time, to me, it seemed like a song about history, and, though the song dated from the turn of the century, I was later surprised to realise that the West Clare had only finally closed five years before I arrived in Kilkee

It is a witty song, written to be performed, and Dermott Dunleavy was a master at delivering its every nuance, with phrases like: "the fire's taytotally out", "and while you're breaking bits of trees" and "Have ye got the parcel there for Mrs White?" enunciated for perfect impact.

The whole lounge joining in with the chorus:

"Are ye Right there, Michael, are ye right?
Do ye think that we'll be there before the night?
Sure it all depends on whether,
The old engine holds together......."

would be followed by the Judge's quietly sung:

"And it might, now, Michael, so it might!"

with a wink and a twinkle in the eye.

There would be a sweep of the arm to encourage a joining in with the chorus, and then a wee gesture calling for quiet again to appreciate the verse. He played the lounge like a musician plays his instrument and it was a pleasure to be part of the experience.

Dermott Dunleavy would have a hard shift on the bench in Dundalk in the next few years, as the Troubles erupted, and he found himself dealing with numerous "cross-border" incidents – but, by all accounts he retained his sense of humour and dramatic awareness. He later received an appointment in Wexford where he continued to be famous for his wit and judgements – once even breaking into song on the bench. He could be particularly harsh on establishments breaking licensing laws, and their effect on young people's drinking, so it is maybe not surprising that he liked to remain in the residents' lounge at the Hydro, safe from any embarrassing involvement in late night lock ins elsewhere!

Like so much of my Hydro experiences, my innocence of Irish affairs at the time led to later fascinating discoveries. I only recently found out that Dermott was a native of Mohill, in my family's county of

Leitrim. Furthermore, he had established a Drama Group of some renown there – The Breffni Players, and throughout his life was acclaimed for his performances of Percy French songs – which explained the impact he had in the Hydro's lounge. He died in May 2006, and I regret I had not discovered the Leitrim connection sooner. I would loved to have thanked him for those entertaining nights in the Hydro lounge, which still resonate, some fifty years later.

The Hydro was run by a company called "Western Hotels" and I can recollect the company name on the hotel's distinctive red lettered stationery; I think one of the directors may have been called F.X. Burke. As events have suggested, the hotel, or the company was clearly struggling by the late sixties – though to discover it was not opening one year – possibly 1971 – was a huge shock and disappointment.

As a holidaymaker, it seemed to me a successful enterprise; I certainly loved staying there. However, I suspect it needed investment which perhaps the company did not possess. Holiday choices were changing, more people were using Kilkee for day trips or weekend breaks, rather than long summer vacations; even the dance halls were not drawing the revenue they once had. The spread of cars and more spending power meant more folk had their own transport and found it easier to take a lodge for the month, rather than pay for the expense of an hotel.

In the final year, the company put in a kind of "hands on" manager to "assist" Barbara Weldon. Of course, I know nothing of the machinations behind this idea, but when we arrived that August we discovered the lively presence of Brian Fitzsimons. He was a Dublin lawyer, apparently, and charged with making sure the Hydro turned a profit that season.

He was hugely sociable and got to know all the guests very quickly, and his major skill was being able to produce platters of chicken sandwiches at 3 a.m. Whether he was successful in his remit, I do not know, but, when we attempted to book the following year, we were told the Hydro would not be re-opening.

It was hard to be in Kilkee the following year and see the hotel closed, given the happy times that had been spent there. The place kind of stuttered on for a few years. For a while the Ballroom still operated, and on occasions the bar was functioning. I even stayed there once more when it was briefly operating as an hotel again a few years later.

But, of course, it was not the same: it couldn't be. The town had changed and I had changed, and you can't bring back the past. It was obviously in a poor state of repair and largely understaffed. I believe it operated for a time as a kind of hostel for the workmen who were building the ESB power station at Moneypoint on the Shannon.

Eventually, the Ballroom was demolished – part of the dance floor going to the dancing area of the Bar at the Royal Marine Hotel, and the entire building was converted into "Old Moore's Holiday Apartments".

Every time one of the apartments is advertised for sale, the thought strikes me that it would be nice to own a piece of the old Hydro, but, if I'm honest, the memories mean much more than bricks, mortar, and plasterboard. We should recognise that, for well over a hundred years, "Moore's", "Old Moores", and the Hydro, catered for a certain type of holiday and established a special place in the hearts of thousands of visitors: the young, the old and the young at heart. But, perhaps, its time as an hotel had run its course. The times were changing, Kilkee was changing, and holidays were changing. As the world of teenagers developed, as marketing raised expectations, and as communications meant more of the world was in holiday reach, perhaps the closure of the Hydro was in some ways inevitable. However, while its doors were open, it really was a special place.

I regularly fell in love there, I experienced in full the joy of being young and free and on holiday. On the post board I saw the telegram bearing my last school exam results, and I could take you to the exact spot on the front lawn where I stood overlooking the bay to find out whether or not I was headed for university. My thinking was quite simple: I wanted to be alone when I opened the results, and, if they were disappointing, I wanted that fabulous view ahead of me, to remind me that the world was still a beautiful place. When I opened the envelope, the results were what I needed, and I looked out – over the strand, the waves, the pier and George's Head, and I said a prayer of thanks. What a wonderful world!

I am delighted to have been able to record for posterity what it was like to stay at this most distinctive of hotels, and to describe happy times spent there, but, as the Beatles sang at the end of their own sixties' adventure, in the end, it really is better to just "Let it Be."

"ON THE FLOOR, THE PEOPLE DANCE AROUND….."

When folk ask you to name your favourite song or favourite book, the answer is never certain. It is always difficult to confine your answer to one title – it depends on your mood at the time the question is asked, the criteria you are going to use in your choice. Do you choose the most skilfully written, or the one you enjoyed most, or a title which meant a lot to you at a certain time in your life?

In reality, there is no one answer – it can vary according to circumstances – which I suppose is one reason for social media's fascination with "lists" – giving you the space to make multiple rather than single choices.

So, I'm afraid I can't point to one particular facet of Kilkee which made me fall in love with the town; the reasons are many and varied.

However, if you were to ask me which aspect of my holiday experience had the most immediate impact on me, I would unhesitatingly say: "The Hydro Ballroom".

At this stage, a generation or more after their heyday, writing about the showbands and the importance of the ballrooms, is a difficult business. They have sunk far enough into the past to have become part of the 'nostalgia industry', and, as a result, descriptions of the period and the consensus on what it was like, have become rather stylised and inaccurate.

For anyone born in the 70s or later, "showband dance" must summon up an automatic picture of cabaret type performances, often top heavy with schmaltzy country and Irish tunes, sung by people with bad hair and an outlandish sense of fashion. Perhaps that just reflects any generation's view of their parents' and grandparents' musical tastes – but the fact remains that, in the sixties, the ballrooms and the showbands were far more than that stereotypical view suggests.

There were, of course, sound musical and socio-economic reasons why the dance orchestra scene of the 1940s and 50s morphed into the showband craze of the following decade, and they are, I would suggest, uniquely Irish.

After independence and the isolationist policies followed by De Valera in particular, there must have been, particularly in rural Ireland which still made up the majority of the country's population, a feeling of wanting to get a glimpse through a scarcely opened door of all that was going on elsewhere in Europe. Irish radio and television was slow in coming, especially away from the east coast, where at least giant aerials could allow some degree of "eavesdropping" on UK outlets.

Work hours were long, income low, and, outside of family and neighbourhood gatherings, entertainment was scarce for many people across the country. A ballroom, often in the beginning controlled by the parish, was a way of bringing people together from surrounding townlands, a chance to meet friends away from the land and everyday concerns, a bit of glamour, if you like. As the statistics relate, for a time, more than half of rural married couples had originally met in the dancehall – and if this seems strange to today's generation, a visit to the hill farms in the west of Ireland, with their preponderance of elderly bachelors, will underline the need for a chance to socialise and meet with the opposite sex, in times when rural isolation was far more insurmountable than in today's more interconnected world.

Former Taoiseach, Albert Reynolds and his brother, along with promoters like Jim Hand, recognised the chance to make money by modernising the scene, taking control away from the clergy, and providing larger, more well appointed, venues, where folk from a number of towns could meet and dance to modern music. They would steal an idea from the picture houses of earlier in the century, and provide, at least superficially, venues which were 'glamorous' and, often literally, star filled, with their mirrorballs and bright designs: an alternative to the daily grind. In areas where there were few shops or opportunities to buy the latest records, very often the showband dance was people's only chance of hearing the 'top ten' music of the day.

So, for today's hipsters who see the showbands as outmoded and old fashioned even in their time – you should know that they brought glamour to all parts of the land, and offered popular music and a chance to socialise – and that meant the ballroom could be an exciting and vital part of the community – for all ages, but particularly for the young. The bands, like circus performers, had the attraction of being here today and gone tomorrow. The halls took on the character of the area in which they were built – and in seaside resorts like Kilkee, Ballybunion, Salthill, Tramore and the rest, there was a special atmosphere as the brass section blared out the introduction to the night's entertainment, and a thousand holiday romances began to dance to the rhythm.

Of course, as a fourteen year old arriving in Kilkee, I knew nothing of this history. In fact, you could say I found the showband dance by accident almost.

Early on during my first visit, one of the receptionists pointed out to us that there were table tennis tables, bats and balls available down in the ballroom. Without that information, I may never have got around to visiting the hall, but we were keen to play, and a few of us went to investigate.

We soon developed a keen, and competitive daily table tennis habit in the empty and echoing dancehall, but my attention was directed towards the stage.

As a fourteen year old, I had still not attended my first 'live' concert nor had I managed to get to any of the "discotheques" which were starting to be popular at home. In truth, the idea of a "dance" seemed mysterious and adult, and, frankly, terrifying to me. After all, there would be girls there!

On the other hand, I went to school around five miles away from the famous "Cavern". Like all my peers, I was enthralled by the Beatles and the mid sixties pop charts, so what I saw on the Hydro Ballroom stage fascinated me.

The closest I had ever been to 'live pop music' was watching on television, so, between table tennis games, when I saw the showband paraphernalia, I was fascinated: amps, speakers, microphones and instruments were laid out on the stage, ready for the night's performance.

Back in the fifties the Hydro had employed a "resident dance band" for the summer season; at one point it was Johnny McMahon and his orchestra; but by the mid sixties, their preference was to rotate the bands on more or less a weekly basis. This helped to build crowds when a band was popular, and kept down costs because there was the potential for a night without a dance, often a Monday. For the bands involved, sometimes semi-professional, it was a chance to come down to Kilkee for a summer holiday with their family, staying perhaps on a caravan site or one of the guest houses, and have their expenses paid by playing each night.

As a result, in those innocent days, they often left their gear on the stage from night to night. As the only people with access to the dance hall during the day would be hotel staff and guests, the equipment was thought to be safe.

So I became fascinated by this pop music gear laid out so accessibly, and, inevitably, wondered about seeing the band in action. This interest was further fuelled by the buses or vans which every showband had. They were a variety of vehicles, obviously needing to convey seven or eight band members and gear around the country, and always with copious advertising, featuring the band's name, scattered all over it. At one point it would be a competition to see how many bandwagons you could spot on the road if heading to Dublin from the west in late afternoon.

At Kilkee, I remember, the Carousel had a VW Camper van, and Kevin Flynn and the Editors and the Vanguard Six had converted buses. The sight of them parked outside the Ballroom would heighten excitement for that night's dance.

Curiosity aroused, we started to discuss the dances. Maybe, we thought, we could go to the dance just to watch the band – if we were all together we could avoid the embarrassment of actually "dancing", whatever that meant. It should be remembered that, in the mid sixties, "dancing" was in the throes of a revolution, where modern dancing – which was basically just moving one's body in time to the beat, was still competing with formal "ballroom dancing" – the waltz, the foxtrot and even jiving – as to the "proper" way of dancing. We were aware, boys and girls, quite apart from our shyness with the opposite sex, we might not even know "how" to dance! Most of us in the hotel gang attended single sex schools and were hesitant about dealing with the opposite sex in such a setting.

However, we decided "going to watch" might be "good fun".

So that is how we started going to the dance in the ballroom. We would gather in a group near the stage, watch the band, sing along, ask for a few requests, and generally enjoy the music.

Of course, inevitably, the urge to dance overtook us and we worked out, without ever discussing it, that if we danced only with each other, the embarrassment of rejection or mockery would be avoided. In time, we graduated to including any hotel staff who were there as our potential partners.

It is probably about time to describe the dancehall, its atmosphere and the routines of the showband dance in a little more detail for younger readers!

You entered the Hydro Ballroom up a flight of steps from the street, turning to the right half way up, to pass a small box office. Once inside, there was a lounge area, for couples to "sit out" with low tables and easy chairs, and to your left there were folding full length doors, essentially the back wall of the ballroom, which were normally open on to the dance floor itself.

If you walked to the end of the lounge and turned left you would reach the mineral bar – soft drinks only - and a cloakroom.

Standing at the back of the dance hall, as many, including the local Guards on duty, often did, this would be your view:

The hall was long, oblong and high roofed. At the far end was the stage – a fair size, but a little cramped for a band of eight and their equipment. The walls were a kind of indeterminate white or cream colour. To your right would be that soft drinks bar and cloakroom and a corridor which led to the hotel and to the gents. The dividing door was normally locked once the dance began, but, as hotel residents, we had free admission, and tended to arrive early before the door was closed. That corridor is one of my major memories of the dances – a bizarre mix of stale alcohol and toilet disinfectant – which should be nauseating but is actually redolent of good times!

There were two double door fire exits in the left hand wall, which were often opened when it became too hot inside. At the top of the hall on the right was the Ladies' – which also served as a dressing room, in which the bands would don their "showband suits" before taking the stage. If suits and synchronised dance movements seem hideously old fashioned now, it should be remembered that, at this time, in the sixties, that was what the Beatles were still doing. Stage gear was important to the showbands for most of the era – a hangover from the old dance orchestras, I suppose, and many bands developed a recognisable signature style. As a result of this, the first 'made to measure' suit I ever had, possibly for a family wedding, was a brown, shiny, showband suit, in which I thought I looked "smooth" – and ready to leap on stage as a substitute vocalist should the need ever arise. In this I was much like a small child wearing his team's football kit to the game and hoping to be called on to the pitch. I am very happy to report, though, that I never once wore the suit to a dance! Luckily my favourite bands did not include The Indians – who dressed in buckskin and feathered head dresses, or Eileen Reid and the Cadets, who dressed as sailors!

There was a basic lighting rig, and a mirrorball in the centre which sometimes worked. Once the dancehall was busy, the main lights would be dimmed and the light source would be the stage lights. It was hugely atmospheric.

Though the dance would be advertised as beginning at 9pm, very few would arrive at that time: the bars in town would be far more attractive. On the other hand, the group of us from the hotel would head for the hall as soon as we heard the band tuning up. After all, we had convinced ourselves we were primarily going to see the band rather than to dance.

In those times, a showband generally consisted of a vocalist, drummer, guitarist, bass player, keyboards and a brass section of two or three. If you were the singer, you had got the gig because you could hold a tune and you were considered to have some kind of 'stage presence' – the 'face' of the outfit – though, to be fair a good few vocalists also played guitar. For the rest, musical ability and flexibility was key. Keyboards could often double up on lead or rhythm guitar, or even brass, and, among a brass section, two or three could probably cover alto and tenor sax, trumpet, trombone, flute and clarinet. In the days before tape loops or even synthesisers, if you were to replicate the sound of a hit record, you needed that kind of musical range.

My friends at home would be cynical about the showbands and their lack of original material, but I never ceased trying to convince them of their musical excellence.

I had seen this first hand on my first visit to Kilkee.

If I was around the hotel and I spotted the band coming in to rehearse in the afternoon, I would go down to the ballroom to watch and to chat with the band members. One of my favourite bands were the Carousel from Crumlin in Dublin, who were managed by Peter Lawless. Their vocalist, Billy McDonnell, was very chatty, as were most of the musicians.

On one occasion I was there when the manager arrived with a new single, just released and climbing the charts. I may be wrong, but my memory suggests it was the Mamas and Papas' hit: "Monday Monday", which was a complicated mix of harmonies and instrumentation. They had a small record player, on which they repeatedly played the disc, whilst the various members of the band sought to work out their parts.

Within an hour they had listened to the record, worked out their parts, started to put it together, and ended up playing a fine representation of the single which they would replicate that night. It was, by any standards, an impressive piece of musicianship – and you had to remember, they played from 9 till 2am each night, with the setlist which that involved.

Later on, bands like the Times and the Freshmen started to write their own original material, but even when copying chart sounds, the showbands could be professional, talented, and exciting.

To fully evoke the atmosphere in the hall, I should also explain how the dances were arranged – for that formed the shape of the experience.

In what was presumably a hangover from the more formal "dance orchestra" days, the bands played "sets" of three or four songs at a time. Given they played for five hours, this gave them a brief break every fifteen minutes or so, as well as a space for a change of instruments if needed.

The vocalist or band leader would announce: "That's all for now, folks, your next dance, please" – then there would be a two minute break before they struck up with the next song. A set would be composed of either "fast" songs or "slow" songs, which would, of course, determine the type of dancing.

It is easy to understand the benefits to the band from this arrangement – but it also influenced the dancers in different ways.

As a boy, once you had asked a girl to dance and been accepted, you would normally have three or four songs in which to impress her with your dancing ability or "power of personality", which was better than having to bowl her over in the time of one song! It would be unusual if a girl or boy excused themselves before the end of the set, if they did, you could believe that there really was no possibility of chemistry between them. When that happened – and - given all the other couples would be remaining on the floor, it was quite obvious, - the girl would usually head for the Ladies, while the boy would swagger back to his pals, attempting to look unworried. For both it was acutely embarrassing.

There was method involved in this type of dance arrangement. Between each song there was time for some basic chat, and then a decision to be made – by either partner - at the end of the set. If you initiated a conversation after the last song, and if your partner stayed put, you would still be on the dance floor when the next song started, and the assumption was that you would keep dancing. If the next set was a "slow" set, then you would have even more chance of chatter or romance. Timing was everything!

At the end of the set you might also ask if your partner wanted to go for a "mineral", and that would be a chance to sit outside in the lounge and chat, before coming in to dance again to a song you both liked.

However, if you had not enjoyed the experience and wanted to dance with somebody else, there was an urgency about your hurried: "Thank you" at the end of the set, so you could make your escape.

Given the prevailing attitudes of the times, it was actually an arrangement which gave the girl some unusual power – to refuse to dance, or to escape from a clumsy or irritating partner, or to indicate that she was willing to keep dancing.

If this sounds very civilised, I should maybe provide a more general description of what was happening around the star struck couple.

We should remember that, though the Hydro was a hotel ballroom in a seaside town, around the country, especially in more rural parts, it was often the only way of a boy meeting a girl and vice versa. It further afforded a chance for mixed company outwith the gaze of family and neighbours, which away from the dancehall was not often possible. So, without too much exaggeration, you could say there was an atmosphere of slight desperation sometimes.

In a society where the Church laid down the rules, relationships with the opposite sex could be fraught with worry and, often, subterfuge. The physical positioning of boys and girls in the hall reflected this.

In the Hydro, most of the girls would be sitting or standing along the far wall, on the opposite side to the bar and cloakroom. Facing them from the other side, in front of the bar, were the massed ranks of the lads.

If you were a couple, or had come in a group of acquaintances, you escaped the pressures of this arrangement. For the others, it was like some kind of social science experiment.

The lads smoked, narrowed their eyes like John Wayne, and talked to their pals out of the side of their mouths, while trying to catch the eye of a girl they liked. It would be fair to say, unless they were pioneers, many had a fair amount of Dutch courage taken on board.

The boys who were most shy would be standing at the back, looking like they wished they were anywhere else, and hoping to spot a girl who seemed as lost as them on the far side of the hall.

The girls either stood in groups, eyeing the boys and making comments to each other which inevitably ended up with laughter or screams, or sat on the benches along the wall, hoping the boy they liked would notice them and be brave enough to ask them to dance. Occasionally, as if at a hidden signal, a group of five or six girls would grab their bags and head for the Ladies, crossing the hall, walking between and around the dancers on the dance floor, like travellers negotiating an airport departures lounge.

Naturally, at the end of each set, there was the ebb and flow of dancers returning to their original side of the hall. Then, when the band announced the next set – and whether it would be fast or slow – there would be a wave of boys heading across towards the girls. This was always a moment worth watching, and I suppose it involved some of the elements of soldiers going 'over the top'.

The choice of girl and the decision to ask her to dance was seldom an impetuous thing. The lad may have known her already, have been watching her dance earlier, or have been building up his courage for the big moment.

As a result, when the band announced the start of the next set, there would be a surge of movement from the area where the boys were grouped. Like a charge out of the trenches, there would be every method employed to reach safely the other side of "no man's land". Some proceeded heedless of all around them, eyes fixed on the object of their affection, knocking bystanders out of the way. Others became unaccountably swivel eyed and beat a tortuous path to the girl with whom they wanted to dance, as if they had suddenly noticed her at the last moment.

There were those who valued the appearance of poise, who would slowly sashay across the floor like gunslingers preparing for a showdown – a brave technique which sometimes ended in disappointment when the object of their attentions had already been taken up to dance by the time they reached her.

In such an event, or if nerves failed at the last moment, the coping mechanism was either to keep on walking, as if you were on a tour of the hall, or turn to the next available girl and ask her to dance, as if that had been your intention all along. It was all about saving face – and woe betide the guy who made the wrong call, and was roundly abused by his 'second choice'.

I have described the situation 'tongue in cheek' here, with references to the trenches and the wild west – and it is easy to do so from the safe refuge of fifty years later.

However, it is fair to say that for the less confident – of both genders, it could be a nerve wracking experience.

As is always the case for teenagers, peer pressure exaggerated every moment. Girls faced the agonising wait to see if anyone would ask them to dance – a kind of public judgment. These days we would talk of the need for equality and girls to be supported in being assertive – but such views were far from accepted in the mid sixties. In addition, it was not always the case that girls received 100% support from their friends – there was competition in winning the best looking boys, and jealousy could also rear its ugly head. Some girls experienced uncomfortable situations because they were too polite to say no to a dance request, or to cut a set short. They also suffered from the attentions of more than a few lads who had drink taken.

There was, every now and then, a set which was called as a "Ladies' Choice" – when the girls got to reverse the process and cross the floor to ask a lad to dance – but somehow it never seemed as powerful a moment as when it was the boys' turn, though there would have been lads as scared of being asked as they were of having to ask.

It was a long walk across the floor for a boy – his mates watching from behind him, the girls lined up opposite, all waiting to see who he would ask to dance, both genders ready with a quip or a telling phrase. The embarrassment caused by a refusal, or by the girl's friends giving out a good slagging, put off many boys from dancing, and there were more than a few who stood all night mocking their pals without making any attempt to dance themselves.

These, however, were the extremes of the dance hall experience. For most, it was an enjoyable social outing. Many came to the dance as a couple and many as part of a group – like my friends and I from the Hydro.

The hall had an atmosphere all of its own, which could change from hour to hour and night to night – depending on the dancers and the band.

In some ways I enjoyed the first hour or so the best, given my interest in music and bands. The musicians were more relaxed in that hour, with only a few people in the hall. They played new songs that they were still polishing, and sometimes individual musician's favourites which would not fit into the sets later.

At this time, the showbands had discovered the Binson echo chamber. This early 'effects' machine gave depth to the music being played – especially vocals, and gave a more "produced" tone – which, of course, helped the bands reproduce the sound of the original recordings.

The empty hall exacerbated the effect and made that first hour quite atmospheric. We would hang around the stage, get requests played for us, and take the opportunity to watch the musicians closely. It was a bit of an education, for me, at any rate.

In those days, a fair few songs were written about dancing, and if they were played, they would add to the atmosphere. I can remember The Troggs' "With a girl like you", with its final verse:

> "So, before this dance has reached the end,
> To you across the floor my love I'll send,
> I just hope and pray, that I'll find a way to say:
> 'Can I dance with you?' "

And I could not help but identify with the lyric of Herman's Hermits' "My Sentimental Friend":

"On the floor, the people dance around,
Moving close together.
And there, all alone in the corner,
Is a girl I once knew, who broke me in two."

The meaning behind these dance-based lyrics would be hazy or unimportant to today's youngsters, but back then they spoke to direct experience.

Once the hall was full, given the competing styles of dancing, it was remarkable how people managed to dance without causing injury or starting fights.

During a "fast" set, sometimes introduced as a "quick step", you might have couples dancing, facing each other, in "modern style" in the centre of the hall, and at the sides, older, or more formal, couples, dancing round the hall, performing foxtrots, waltzes or even sambas, depending on the beat of the song being played. The men who were leading basically had to steer their partners around and around, avoiding flailing arms and strutting bodies, whilst, presumably, attempting to murmur sweet nothings. To add to the general unpredictability, there would sometimes be a couple jiving frantically – attracting their own small circle of admirers, or even folk performing versions of the jitterbug. Dancing was a hugely popular hobby and there were many people who were practised and accomplished in many types and variations.

Slow sets were little better in terms of movement.

The experienced and older dancers would perform formal dance steps to match the rhythm – a waltz, perhaps, whilst the younger set, who knew nothing of such steps, more or less stood on the spot, moving gently from side to side, lost in each others' eyes. The potential for the irresistible force to meet with the immoveable object was obvious, particularly if excitement was raised by amorous intentions or drink taken.

It must have looked quite amazing from the stage: a pulsing mass of movement, with eddies of shapes in all directions – especially when the hall was packed and full, as it was frequently in the summer months. The situation might be made even more interesting if a very popular band were playing, and a large group had gathered in front of the stage to watch the singer, unconscious of all that was going on around them.

Another variation came when two girls might decide to dance together, moving confidently round the floor or, with similar effect, when you had a couple who determinedly made their way around, with no apparent awareness of anybody else, as if wearing blinkers.

And then there were Sunday nights.

I have suggested that the view from the stage of the physical movement involved at the height of the dance may have been fascinating. Less obvious, but potentially more powerful, was the emotional content of the Sunday night dance.

Youth can be ignorant and unintentionally cruel, and, without seeking to patronise either my younger self or the dancers, there's no doubt that we lacked the life experience to react totally sympathetically to the specific circumstances of Sunday nights at the Hydro Ballroom.

Sunday was the farmers' 'day off'. Apart from the day of the Mart, it was one of their few opportunities to come in to town and socialise, and so, in the sixties, the personnel at Sunday night dances in the Hydro was different to the rest of the week. This was also the case because many holiday makers travelled to or from Kilkee on Sundays, meaning each week there was a change of population – in the town and in the dancehall, with fewer visitors and more locals.

The idea of the bachelor farmers coming in from the Loop Head peninsula to 'find a wife' at these dances is one which would be easy to satirise or demean, and, as I have said, in our youthful ignorance, we had little understanding of the situation.

Compared to some parts of the west of Ireland, Corca Baiscinn is not particularly isolated – though back in the Sixties it was not as 'connected' as it is now – but isolation can be about more than physical geography.

Farming in west Clare was a difficult occupation, still is, and, as is the case anywhere, tends to involve long hours of hard work. The opportunities for socialising – especially outside the immediate circle of family and neighbours – were limited. The demands of the land, family, heredity, and work could eat up all the available time. The years from 'helping out on the farm' as a young boy, to being the main worker, with added responsibility for elderly parents, could pass quickly and remorselessly, and many a country man, or woman, found themselves looking at fifty and wondering how they got there and what the future would hold for them.

Though it is a stereotype, the demographic attests to its accuracy: for a farmer in late middle age, a younger wife and the possibility of children was a practical boost to the farm and a major boost to his own mental well being. It is fair to say, as well, that there were women who came to the Hydro on those Sunday nights for whom a farmer looking for a wife would be an answer to fears of a future which might involve a lonely life caring for increasingly frail parents and with limited social contact.

Like the status of showbands themselves, for younger people today, this description of the motivation behind those Sunday night dances might appear patronising, stylised, or over exaggerated. However, it needs to be remembered that the expectations in rural Ireland of the 1960s were only slowly changing from those of the 1940s; it was a conservative, traditional, and inward looking society where the roles of men and women were as they had been for most of the past century, and this was demonstrated in respect for the Church and the State and traditional ways of doing things. Below the surface things may have been changing, but in 1966, few were brave enough to take on age old 'certainties', at least in public.

One of the reasons I decided to write this memoir was the seeming absence, at least according to internet search engines, of any detailed description of the Hydro, its ballroom, and its holidays. I felt it would be good to have a record, albeit from one person's point of view, of "what it was like to be there". However, as I was writing, I spotted a link to "Hydro Ballroom" on the Irish Times' site. The paper had done a feature on clergy control of the dance halls from the thirties onwards, and well known Kilkee person, John Williams, had contributed his memories of the Hydro in the 1950s.

Apparently in those days, when the Johnny McMahon Orchestra were in residence, the Parish Priest forbade them to play a "slow dance" as the last tune of the evening. He would walk around the hall with a walking stick, and, if he thought any couples were dancing too closely, would poke the stick between them crying: "Leave room for the Holy Ghost!" In addition, he would wait outside at the end, and if he thought a couple were leaving together, would detain the boy for ten minutes and tell the girl to go straight home.

Thankfully, Canon Kenny never showed his face in the ballroom in the sixties, but John's reminiscences are a reminder of how slowly times changed in Kilkee, and Sunday nights were perhaps a last remnant of earlier times.

Anyone familiar with William Trevor's "Ballroom of Romance" will find it easy to imagine those Sunday nights as being possibly grim affairs with much at stake. The reality, though, was somewhat different. Not all the men and women who came in to the dance on a Sunday night were necessarily desperate for a life partner. Some were happy with their lot and were just there 'for the craic'. There could be the joyous atmosphere represented by a large number of people on their "day off", and many were expert dancers who put on quite a show – especially when contrasted with youngsters like ourselves, for whom dancing meant moving vaguely to the music or shuffling on the spot.

From my perspective, half a century later, one of the most positive aspects of the Hydro Ballroom, rather like the sessions in the hotel's lounge, was the opportunity for folk of all ages to come together for their entertainment. I suppose in the hall there would have been folk from fourteen or fifteen years of age up to those in their late fifties. When we were forging a new "sixties' identity" for ourselves as 'teenagers', I don't think it occurred to us that, whilst we were gaining much in power and visibility as a distinctive grouping, we were also losing some of the closeness to the older generation which had the potential to provide much insight and warmth.

It is a trend which has continued into the social media age – a separation of the generations, and an increasing isolation, despite the apparent virtues of cyber connectivity. We may have smiled at the earnest farmers and their seriously concentrating dance partners, but I like to think it was an affectionate reaction. As the words of the song suggest: "But we were so much older then, we're younger than that now."

The Bands played their part too – and, returning each year, as did many of them, I got to know the musicians. I recall Billy McDonnell of the Carousel, and their summer single "Holiday Romance", Don Cotter, of Kevin Flynn and the Editors, extra cool, with his shoulder length hair and dark glasses, who sang "Death of a Clown" even better than Dave Davies, The Vards, from Cork, Tommy Drennan and the Monarchs from Limerick, The Vanguard Six, The Blue Beats from Ennis – all of whom provided night after night of entertainment, and were happy to chat with a music mad teenager and welcome him to their rehearsals. One year, I had the added treat of watching Granny's Intentions play the Olympia Hall in Merton Square, before going down to the showband dance in the Hydro: a case of having my cake and eating it!

The Hydro dance also lead to one of our more interesting experiences.

There was a band playing in 1969 called "The Vards" from Cork – and they were very good – they did a steaming version of Free's "Alright Now", I recall, and, on the Sunday afternoon, set up their gear at the caravan site and played an impromptu open air gig.

We got friendly with them and were a bit annoyed that they were not getting bigger crowds at the Hydro – so we decided to mount a publicity drive.

Nowadays, of course, this would involve social media, posters professionally produced on the laptop, and maybe even balloons and printed tee shirts. Back in the day, we had pieces of paper and pens, ballpoints that is – not even marker pens - and we wrote: "The Vards, at the Hydro, all week."

We then went out in the middle of the night, and, using sellotape, attached these 'posters' to just about every business, bar and shop wall we could reach in the town.

We were very pleased with our efforts, although, if we had been less naïve, it might have occurred to us that, in a town the size of Kilkee, everybody already knew who was playing at the Hydro, and a tatty piece of paper and its illegible message was unlikely to affect the attendance either way.

The next day, Brian Fitzsimons, the Dublin lawyer and under manager of the hotel, called us all together.

"I know you were only trying to help…" he said, "but I've had every business in the town on to me today complaining about you."

In those days, virtually every building in the town had a frontage of painted stone. When the business people had, understandably, pulled our tatty bits of paper off their premises, because they were sellotaped, the paint had come with them – and they were all faced with a redecoration bill.

I'm not too sure that Brian didn't see the funny side of it, but we were all shamefaced, and, though it reflects well on our enthusiasm for the Hydro and its Ballroom, it was a brilliant example of the road to hell being paved with good intentions!

So all of this, and more, was the impact forged on me by the Hydro Ballroom. Those who attended the dances were a reflection of the society in which they existed – young and old, town and country, local and visiting, traditional and progressive, some looking forward and others looking back.

For me, the dance had the attraction of the new and unknown, it contributed to an advance in my social awareness and, eventually, my self confidence. I used to say to my friends that I did all my growing up for a year in my annual three weeks in Kilkee – with meeting the opposite sex, finding out about new places and backgrounds – and my nights in the Hydro Ballroom. Maybe that was an exaggeration, but not by much!

In my memories, the Hydro Ballroom represents excitement, I suppose. I was always on a high at those dances. Non-stop action for up to four hours ensured the adrenaline was flowing and the endorphins were produced. It was a perfect holiday experience, with worries and stresses banished and different parts of the personality developed – a real case of re-creation! I would come out of the dance each night feeling invigorated – that mix of exercise, music, atmosphere and friendship never failed to boost my spirits.

On reflection, it was a gentle introduction to the idea of romance and relationships – at least for this fourteen year old. It's impossible not to compare it favourably to a later world where the internet, sexting, reality television shows, and social media behaviours bring earlier and overwhelming pressures on young people regardless of how prepared they are for the moment.

One August night at the end of the dance, I was standing on the roadway in front of the Hydro. Around me, folk were getting into cars or walking away towards the town or the strand – their chatter was hanging in the night air. My shirt was cold on my back – the sweat from some serious dance moves!

High above the bay the sky was a luminescent navy blue, dotted with hundreds of sparkling stars. There was a gently warm breeze and a freshness in the night air after the mixed atmosphere of smoke and perfume in the hall.

I stood there, and, as I breathed in the scene, a group of falling stars fell heart stoppingly from deep in the blue, down towards the line of orange lights reflected round the strandline. It was the first time I had seen falling stars and it was achingly beautiful. Everything about the evening came together – and I had a sudden but firm conviction, in that moment, as a teenage boy, with choices still to be made, and the future beckoning, that life was going to be good – and it is wonderful, a lifetime later, to be able to write that my presentiment was proved accurate.

Readers will be as perplexed perhaps as I am to discover I still have perfect recall of small and insignificant moments from those Hydro dances, even a lifetime later. The images are vivid, like Technicolor postcards in a long forgotten album.

I can conjure up the deep brown and cream colours of Don Cotter's Rickenbacker guitar as he sang "Death of a Clown", the blue and black sparkling design on the Premier Drum kits, the in time steps of the brass section, instruments at rest, during a soaring version of "A Poor Man's Roses", the milky white of a Burns bass guitar, a forest of hands in the air as the band sang "Help me Rhonda", the blast of brass and the syncopated movements of the band for the intro to "Help Yourself", "Vehicle" and those Chris Andrews stand outs: "To whom it concerns" and "Yesterday Man".

It is not hard to recapture the slowing in pace that was always achieved by the Jim Reeves' number: "He'll have to go", the mumble of shared conversations in the gap between sets, or the welcome touch of gentle warm evening air as you passed by one of the opened fire doors. I only need to see a 7 Up bottle to recapture the stickiness of the floor around the bar area; and the echo of music in an empty hall - anywhere and anytime - has me back in that big hall overlooking Moore Bay in 1966.

And if that all seems rather fanciful – well, that was the romance of the Hydro Ballroom!

88

THE DUTCH, THE MARINE, THE VIC AND THE STRAND

I suppose the Hydro will always be my "default" hotel, when I think of Kilkee, but, in fact, over the years I have had experience of staying in some of the others in the town, and, even those I have never used have played a role in my Kilkee memories.

It was quite a shock to my mother and I to discover that the Hydro was closed. She had written off in January as normal for our three week booking in August, requesting our usual rooms and indicating how much we were looking forward to our return. When the letter arrived indicating that the Hydro would not be opening that season, we were completely taken aback.

As is the case in most resorts, each year there was frequent discussion of "how the town was doing", the "summer trade" and the financial health of the various hotels. With only a three week stay in August, at the height of the season, it was difficult for us to judge the Hydro's profitability in any meaningful way, and the insertion of a "co-manager" from Dublin the previous year was, I suppose, a hint that things were not going well. However, when you saw the number of guests, the packed ballroom, and the busy bar, you had to think that it was making some kind of reasonable amount.

In addition, over the previous three years or so, there had been some investment –a rebuild of the ballroom entrance, a new bar along the front of the building, the conversion of the old cocktail bar into a steakhouse, as well as a new front porch. Maybe it was a case of rearranging the deckchairs on the Titanic, because I suppose a lot of the hotel was tired looking, and certainly, when I went into the staff quarters – either at the back of the hotel itself or in the old Castle Lloyd in Merton Square, next to the Olympia, they were very bare and basic.

I have no idea if "Western Hotels" owned other establishments which were a drag on its finances, or if they had underinvested in the Hydro over the years, or if, as I have suggested previously, its time for success had merely run out.

Whatever was the case, we were faced with finding a new base for our summer in Kilkee.

I am not sure why, but we ended up staying at the Marine. I suppose it would have been a choice between there and the Victoria.

The place had a different feel to the Hydro. It was smaller and attracted an older, more sedate, crowd, but it was still welcoming and provided a good base for our continued summers in the town. In fact, I suppose, overall, we may have spent more years at the Marine than we did at the Hydro. It was helpful when, a few years after its closure, the Hydro briefly re-opened and I spent a couple of nights there, it felt nothing like it had done previously – and I was able to appreciate the replacement we had found in the Marine: different but still comfortable. This feeling was enhanced when a few of the families we had met at the Hydro also switched to our new lodgings.

At the time we started staying there, the Marine had just built an outdoor swimming pool, which was a very pleasant addition to its facilities. Remarkably, in the summers I visited Kilkee – around ten years of them – I don't think we had more than three or four days of rain and often it was very warm and filled with sunshine. This luck with the weather probably added to my affection for the town!

As was her wont, my mother soon made fast friends with the Manageress at the Marine: Paddy Ryan. Paddy was an imposing young woman, often dressed stylishly and with a joie de vivre about her that made you notice when she came into a room. She walked with a limp and sometimes used a stick, the legacy, I think, of quite a serious car accident. I would say she probably had an interesting back story, but what that was I never found out.

She was always very kind to my mother and I and, in the next few years, when I tended to arrive at the Marine with a group of student friends at odd times of the year, she would be very accommodating in terms of tariffs and arrangements. One year we even got a reduced bill because we helped out in the dining room and in cleaning duties.

Like Barbara Weldon at the Hydro, Paddy was faced with the almost impossible task of maintaining the hotel's profitability whilst adapting to a changing clientele. I think the Marine would have been the hotel of choice for older people – for whom a holiday might have consisted of a read of the paper in the lounge, a walk round the bay, maybe a short car trip in the afternoon and decent food in the evening. This was probably augmented by it being the venue for Golf Club and other organisations' Dinner Dances and celebrations: a demographic which was being lost to the town in general. Overseas opportunities were opening up, even for older folk, without too much expense or travel difficulty; a rash of modern or modernised hotels were appearing around Limerick and Ennis. Retired people with comfortable incomes were becoming more adventurous in their habits.

I only stayed once, and briefly, at the Victoria, and, other than the fact that it was quite pleasant, I cannot recall too much about it. In the caricatured visitors' view of the Kilkee hotels in these years, if the Hydro was 'family fun' and the Marine was 'older and richer' then I suspect the 'Vic' was 'commercial travellers and business folk'. It was a description maybe founded on the hotel's being open all year round for a time and so, naturally, the choice of people who had business in the town or west Clare.

The managers and owners of all three hotels must have found their development difficult in changing times – the more so because they were the largest establishments in the town and were well established in visitors' eyes and memories. They were all around a century old by this point and starting to groan a little at the piecemeal additions which had been foisted on to them to change with the times. The Marine had added the swimming pool and, like the Hydro, a 'steak bar' for non-residents, by the entrance. The Hydro had extended its lounge and bar facilities as well. Ultimately, though, it seemed as if not enough people wanted to spend the necessary sum of money for a two or three week summer holiday in Kilkee when they could be guaranteed new experiences and cheaper accommodation – as well as sun and heat – on overseas package holidays.

Another development was the idea of grandparents spending seaside holiday time with the youngsters while the parents enjoyed a more 'adult' holiday in a European city or resort. Whilst this had always been a Kilkee option – with parents dropping in and out of the lodges at weekends or for a week or so while the grandparents stayed for a month or so with the children, - multiple annual holidays were starting to be popular. This meant that while there might be money for the younger members of the family to have a seaside holiday in Kilkee with their grandparents – as well as enjoying other holidays during the year, the cash didn't run as far as an expensive hotel stay – more likely to a lodge, a guest house or the caravan site.

Of course, these three hotels – and Kilkee – were not alone in experiencing these difficulties in a time of rapid change for the hotel and leisure industries. The saving for many places was a mixture of self catering accommodation and an increase in day trippers or weekenders – which has proved to be much the case in Kilkee.

In the end, the Hydro adapted when its building was converted into holiday flats and my beloved old ballroom was demolished. The 'Vic' was completely flattened and has been replaced by a housing and apartment holiday home development, and the Marine has been through a chain of different owners and existences, going from hotel to apartments and back to hotel again.

Back in the sixties, the other establishments of note in the town were the Strand Hotel the Thomond, the Stella Maris, Bayview, Westcliff and Esplanade guest houses. In the seventies I stayed at the Strand and the Stella Maris and later at the Esplanade when it had also converted to self catering apartments.

Like the 'big three' hotels, each place had its atmosphere and reputation. The Strand was famous for its music nights and sessions, as was the Westcliff, which for a time catered for a young crowd. The Stella Maris was a typical Irish Guest House with a comfortable family atmosphere and good plain food. I spent a week there around Easter of 1972 and had the room over the front door looking out down the length of O'Curry St – a fascinating eyrie from which to watch the town going about its business.

The Thomond always seemed to be filled with holidaying Christian Brothers, who would sit in its long sun lounge looking out balefully across the strandline. Being a pupil in a Christian Brothers' school, it was a part of the Strandline I frequently hurried along!

The one hotel I have not yet referred to is, perhaps, if not the elephant in the room, then the eyesore in the Bay.

You could not miss the Atlantic Hotel. Sited high on the raised ground leading down to the strand steps at the East End, between the pier and Allender's Field, it loomed over the entire bay, as if it had been dropped from some huge spaceship. Nowadays the land between its site and the Golf Club is heavily developed, but in the sixties, apart from the derelict Atlantic Lodge near the boat house at the pier, there was no other building on that side of the road, and only a few bungalows or lodges anywhere in that part of the town. This served to make the brutalist building stand out even more.

It was basically a long rectangle of concrete, with a tower at the town end containing a penthouse suite. The greyness was punctuated by the pastel coloured panels on the balconies which were attached to each room – yellows, oranges, pinks, and blues – which quickly faded in the west coast weather conditions.

Even today – with recent decades of building around the town, the buildings visible around Moore Bay preserve a sense of Kilkee's Victorian heritage. This building, in that context, was just bizarre.

It was built in 1964 by a Dutch company – and forever afterwards was referred to as "The Dutch" by locals. The rumour was that it had been intended for Lahinch, further up the coast, where it may have flourished, as surfers and water sports enthusiasts started to colonise that resort. Refused permission to build there, the story goes, they petitioned Bord Fáilte for another site and, with backing not only from the tourist board, but also from Irish Life, they were 'welcomed' to Kilkee instead.

Initially the hotel attracted folk from far afield who would never normally have heard of Kilkee – the company had two other hotels on the Netherlands' North Sea coast. Maybe they thought a Kilkee holiday would provide a similar experience to that found in those hotels.

Ultimately, it seems that the folk who fancied a holiday in the Atlantic Hotel – and in 1964, when it opened, it was £1 a night, good value even then – did not find what they wanted in Kilkee, or else people who wanted to holiday in Kilkee did not find what they wanted in the Atlantic Hotel.

After three years it was sold – to Associated Ballrooms, who tried to make it profitable, eventually reducing it to a bed and breakfast establishment, which closed down half way through the season, and, ultimately, just opening the former dining area as a disco.

Whatever was tried failed to work, and after less than a decade, the Atlantic was left to fall into dereliction. The likelihood is that more folk squatted in it over the next few years than ever paid to stay there. At one point in the mid 80s, I remember Limerick pirate radio "Big L" broadcasting from the top floor penthouse flat with a huge aerial on the roof.

Apparently the hotel building was bought some time later by a Polish entrepreneur who had plans to regenerate the business, but who had seriously underestimated the amount of cash which would be needed.

So "The Dutch" remained – a haunting presence in the east end of the town, curtains blowing through smashed windows on ruined balconies, like shipwrecked sailors waving for help.

It was eventually sold and then demolished in 1998 – a lifespan of thirty four years, during which it had only been effectively trading as a hotel during around twenty five months.

Even its demolition was attended by the bizarre and out of place discovery of $35,000 in $100 notes hidden in a wall. Alas for the workmen, they were found to be counterfeit, and now who can tell how the fakes got there, or who was unable to return to pick them up?

On the site was built yet another hotel – the Ocean Cove, and a series of holiday apartments, as the Celtic Tiger dipped its feet in the west Clare ocean and brought a building boom to the town, on the back of the Seaside Resort Renewal Scheme, populating the east end as never before – at least at the height of the season.

However, the Lynch company who ran the Cove went under, and, as I write this, the Ocean Cove has been closed for some years and the Kilkee Bay, at the entrance to the town has been open, and shut, and changed owners.

It raises the question: with the magnificence of Moore Bay, the strand and the cliffs, how can hotels on the two best sites in Kilkee – at the East End and the West End – not be successful businesses?

It is a question I have discussed with John Williams and others from the town through the decades; as I write this, it is still being discussed in online forums, and everybody has their own views: holiday fashions have changed, the season's too short, the hotels need to be run by hands on management, not as 'investments', they are too expensive, not exclusive enough, need local staff, need better trained staff.

The fact remains, as is often pointed out, there is not a reasonably sized hotel between Ennis and Loop Head – and, given the tourist boom in spa holidays, gourmet trips, walking adventures along the Wild Atlantic Way, weekending and short breaks, you would wonder why Kilkee's major hotels appear to be cursed.

And maybe that is a relevant point. I am indebted to local historian, Tom Byrne, who pointed out the misfortune of one of Kilkee's original hoteliers, and an early post mistress, Margaret Shannon, who ran a guest house, first in Grattan St, and then the West End Hotel situated at the corner of Wellington Square. Despite successfully running establishments in Kilkee for over fifty years, when Mrs Shannon put her hotel up for sale in 1861 (after an unfortunate murder there in the previous year) she could not find a buyer – and eventually only managed to sell part of the hotel as late as 1875.

I cannot help but come back again to my original premise: that the combination of the times that were in it and the hotels, the visitors' expectations, and what was on offer – all of these things came together in the fifties and sixties, but, as the travel industry moved on, Kilkee was caught between preserving its heritage as a slightly old fashioned resort, and attempting some kind of radical transformation to meet the demands of the late twentieth century.

I am not sure the town has the size or infrastructure to reinvent itself, and I'm fairly certain that the majority of its long term visitors and 'fans' would not wish to see it changed beyond recognition.

The memories remain and the town goes forward, relying on the day trip and weekender trade, and the reduced numbers who still head for the town to enjoy their summer holidays, to sustain its existence.

Each generation throws up its civic minded, hard working, visionaries such as, currently, Cillian Murphy, the Haughs and the Redmonds – and the many recent awards won by Loop Head Tourism and others show that there is still life in the old "Queen of the West"!

FOLK YE DON'T MEET EVERY DAY

Through the years I have either written, spoken or thought about Kilkee on a more or less daily basis. On the wall of my Deputy Headteacher's office in school, I had a large panorama of Moore Bay, probably eight or nine photographs wide. It was taken from the lawn in front of the Hydro and showed the bay from the West End over to the Golf Club.

If I was feeling stressed or under pressure, I would often take time out to gaze at the pictures and complete an imaginary walk around the bay. I would start on the road outside the old Atlantic Lodge, pass the derelict Dutch and the Intrinsic's recovered anchor, and veer to my right past the Thomond Hotel, taking care to avoid the gaze of the holidaying Christian Brothers. I would continue past the Strand and O'Connell St, past the luminous turquoise of the Esplanade, along the Strandline, and on to the picture window at the back of Egan's, and the Arcadia sign high on the flaking white paint of the picture house. Carrying on between Wally's amusements and the Bandstand, I would pass the old school house advertising bingo, and the long low lodge where the Sheils, garage people from Ennis, would spend their summers. Then it was on to the Vic, Murphy's Café and Bakery with its wonderful cakes, and on to Marine Parade past the public toilets, where I first learned the meaning of 'Fir' and 'Mna', past the lodge where the Nolans lived, to the top of Geraldine Place with its old signpost pointing down to the Methodist Church, and the West End Stores with its Leadmore Dairies and HB ice cream adverts.

Inevitably I would pause to sit on the wall over the racquets alleys and reminisce while I looked up at the Hydro.

Then I would move on, past the West End Hotel and Clar Elagh with its croquet hoops, and round the corner at Edmond Point in front of Sykes's House. Taking care to step over the rubber pipe which took sea water to and from the private swimming pool in the lodge raised above the road here, I would pass the Westcliff Guest House, Dunearn, Newfoundout, Dickie Harris's place, and St Anthony's, one of the final lodges, before heading downhill to Haugh's Pitch and Putt.

I would look out over the Pollock Holes towards George's Head and then make my way up past the Amphitheatre and through the breezeblock wall and on to the fake cobbles built by MGM in 1968 to provide access to the cliffs for the camera crews when filming the "Ryan's Daughter" storm scenes. Looking down at the waves in Intrinsic bay with the usual awe, I would head towards the sheep shelter and then choose between a steep walk up to Lookout Hill and its wonderful views, or a walk down the steps to the Diamond Rocks – for me, the most reflective place on earth. Gazing on Bishop's Island nearly every problem is solved, every concern muted.

This "walk" never failed to help me cope with work pressures, and I occasionally 'shared it' with distressed pupils – which is how there come to be generations of Scots youngsters who have been soothed by the magic of Kilkee – without ever being within a hundred miles of the place!

However, one thing I have been aware of consistently is the danger of "mythologizing" Kilkee and its residents.

As this memoir makes abundantly clear, I love the town and its people in a quite uncritical manner – why would I not? It represents the happiness of youth, family, friends and discovery; it provided me with a link to my own family background and my first experiences of Ireland. There is much about Kilkee which is special to me.

Probably for that reason, I don't want to present an unreal version of a living place, and a place about which, in all honesty, I have a limited knowledge. My connections to the town go back half a century, it is true, but my understanding of the place will always be, *must* always be, from the point of view of a visitor, an outsider.

I have spent time in the town outside of the holiday season and, in so doing, I have maybe seen the place without its summer finery, but the most time I have ever spent in Kilkee during a calendar year would be around seven or eight weeks. I have never been a resident in the town, and the knowledge I have of its people is no more than scratching the surface. That's why this memoir is that of a holidaymaker who loves the town – not a "Kilkee person".

I remember being told of a couple who, like myself, had fallen in love with Kilkee over many years. They were desperate to move to the town and live there, and, when they retired, they grabbed the opportunity with all possible speed, and, during the summer, moved into a bungalow near the old railway station. When I asked how they had settled in, I was told: "They were gone by Christmas!"

In any relationship, it is crucial to understand what makes it work, and, for me, I believe I need Kilkee to be a place I can go to, physically and mentally, rather than "home". That's not to say I have not considered the possibility of a holiday home in the town – especially when the economic situation was most grim for them and buying a property in the town might have been helpful rather than depressing to the economy – but even had I made that commitment, I would still have been a visitor, and I have come to the understanding that our current relationship is what suits us both. Indeed, it is part of the attraction – absence does, after all, make the heart grow fonder. I lived for a time as a child in a seaside town, my wife was born in one, and I am familiar with the difference between holiday season attraction and all year round reality. I love Kilkee in all seasons – but that does not equate with wanting to live there, and, in any case, when I may have found the money to consider a property purchase, I had a family to consider, for whom a house in Kilkee was not a priority!

So, as I move on to write about some of the people of the town, I do so with a clear indication that these were largely folk who acted in the 'soap opera' of my Kilkee days. Some I got to know reasonably well, given my 'part-time status', most were names I could put to faces and little more. Of course, that did not stop me from knowing who they were, but that was based on the thinnest of acquaintance. They peopled my holidays, and I was grateful for that, but it would be pushing it to call them friends, or to suggest I knew much about them. For all that, I have carried their memories with me for half a century, and they played, to a greater or lesser extent, an important part in my youth, whether they knew it or not.

Apart from hotel staff, to whom I have already made reference, the first Kilkee resident I got to know was Barry O'Halloran. I hooked up with him because my mother became friendly with his mother, Peg, a widow also, who ran a small shop on the Circular Rd. She told my mother she had a son around the same age as me, and we eventually met each other.

It was a happy meeting. At the time, Barry and I had similar political views and also shared an interest in music. He would have been one of the more "radical" thinkers in Kilkee at the time, I suppose, and was very community orientated. I enjoyed some good times with him, including an epic 21st Birthday weekend when his pals came across from TCD and appeared to have wreaked havoc all along the old N7. He also took me out on a boat for the lobster pots once in Rinevella Bay on an atmospheric, mist shrouded morning.

Through Barry, I discovered Pearse Fennell's Bar in Carrigaholt and also Tommy Mangan's in Kilrush. Great fun was had there, where lock ins were both traditional and legendary. Tommy reckoned if there was a late knock at the front, you should check under the door: brown shoes got you in, black shoes caused panic as it might be the Sergeant. The escape out of Tommy's through the back was epic as he owned a big Alsatian dog. I was never sure whether it was very friendly or quite vicious, but as we headed out the back and scaled the wall, it would be jumping and barking and growling and you would be lucky to escape with your trousers intact.

It was after one such escape, when we had all gathered on the pavement opposite the pub to wait for the squad car's departure that a Guard slowed the car, wound down a window and said in all seriousness: "Ah come on now, lads. If ye want to be standing there, ye'll need to be moving on!" Happy times indeed!

Best of all, Barry was not one to play along with false impressions. It was thanks to him I probably first recognised the crucial difference between the idealised view of Kilkee, that I might have taken, and the reality of the town which, of itself, is enough to make the place quite special.

Barry went on to work at RTE, on the 'Today Tonight' programme, eventually became involved in the setting up of the channel's teletext service Aertel, and, I understand, later ran his own company.

It was through Barry I met John Williams, whose pharmacy and hardware store on the Circular Rd was a long time staple of business in the town. Like Barry, John's politics were radical for the time and the two combined to publish an excellent magazine for the peninsula, called "Iorrus" after its ancient name. It contained political and cultural articles and was strong on the idea of cooperativism. In many ways it was far ahead of its time, especially given the community based developments all over Corca Baiscinn these days, and showed great awareness of important issues in the area.

John needs no introduction or description from me. Anyone who knows Kilkee will know of John and his huge contribution over a lifetime to the town, and the area, through the Chamber and the Civic Trust, alongside Elizabeth's involvement in the twinning arrangements with Plouhinec in Brittany. Through the years he has always been willing to listen to my views on Kilkee and my declarations of love for the place, and consistently friendly in his forebearance from pointing out I don't really know what I'm talking about! With a family connection to the town for generations, he is a classic example of the civic mindedness upon which small towns depend for their development, and I am sure the folk of Kilkee must appreciate that. I have always felt privileged to have met and known him.

Earlier on, I mentioned that the first Kilkee person we met was P.J. King, who drove the taxi which picked us up from Shannon on our first visit. At this distance it seems quite incredible that we would contemplate three weeks in Kilkee without having a car, but that's the way things were in those days. Because of that, we became dependent on P.J. to take us places – often with a group of pals in addition to my mother and I. With us all crammed into his Ford, singing our hearts out to any tune that came to mind, we would visit places like Killaloe, the Cliffs of Moher, the Burren, the Aillwee Caves, White Strand at Doonbeg, and Bunratty. He was innovative in the trips he guided: once we had tea at Dromoland Castle, and, as a friend of the lightkeeper, he got us up to the light at Loop Head long before it was opened to the public.

After the release of "Ryan's Daughter", it was P.J. who drove us down to Kerry, out past Dingle, to the schoolhouse on the cliff, and up the mountain of Carhoo to see the remains of the street built for the village of Kirrary. He took in Lady's View as well, and also inspired a huge love of the Dingle Peninsula which has never left me.

He was an unassuming and obliging man who became a good friend to us in the years we spent our summers in Kilkee. We were delighted when he married Anna, who had been a receptionist at the Hydro, and then took up a position as postmaster at Lisdeen just outside of Kilkee.

Years later, I was having my evening meal in the dining room of the Strand Hotel, watching a typically dramatic Kilkee sunset over the bay; it really did seem as if the sea was on fire. Across my line of vision passed a couple with a small child who, as in many generations before, was walking, with some parental support, along the top of the low sea wall. I realised it was P.J. and Anna.

In an ideal world, I would have run from the hotel and thanked P.J. for his original welcome to the town, and his kindness to my mother and I. In reality, I finished my meal, pleased to see that Kilkee had delivered yet anther happy ending. It is satisfying to see good people finding happiness.

I have said that I could not claim these folk as friends to whom I was particularly close, but what Barry, John, and P.J. provided were familiar faces each time I returned to Kilkee – giving that feeling of recognition and connection which all returnees crave.

However, if one person represented Kilkee for me for the best part of the fifty years since I first arrived in the town, it would have been Maureen Haugh.

I have recounted how, on my first day in Kilkee, I had explored the West End almost as far as Newfoundout. I had spotted the pitch and putt course at the bottom of the hill but had not been brave enough to go any closer.

On the second day, braver and more at home, I headed out to explore the West End.

There was a weather beaten shop there, more of a shed really, with a lopsided caravan behind it. It was placed in front of what looked to me like a miniature golf course.

I knew nothing of Pitch and Putt, but, living less than a mile from the Royal Birkdale Golf Course in northern England, I was interested in golf, though I had never played it. I wondered if this would be a way to try it out.

Even at 14, I was a shy child, especially with adults, and I am still faintly surprised that I summoned up the nerve to enter the shop.

There was little space, filled with a counter, and behind it shelves of sweets and chocolate bars and soft drinks. A rather forbidding elderly man was to one side, (referred to later by locals as "Pa Haugh"!) but it seemed a younger couple were running the place.

I bought a chocolate bar while I formulated my request to play on the course. As she took my money, the woman said: "Do ye fancy a round on the pitch and putt?" and I nodded gratefully. It was a positive first meeting with Maureen Haugh – and it set the trend for the rest of our encounters.

She took my money and, as I walked towards the back door of the shop, handed me two clubs, a ball, a small scorecard, a couple of plastic tees, and a stubby pencil. I must have looked lost, because, as I went through the door, she said: "Bernie will show you the ropes."

And that was how I met Bernie and Maureen Haugh and played my first ever round of pitch and putt.

I was hooked from the start. God knows how many strokes it took me that first day, but posting a "record" score became an obsession for me and for the rest of that holiday, and for many years to come, it would be an unusual day if I didn't play at least two rounds, carefully recording my score, hole by hole.

I suppose it would be a normal occupation for a child who was fairly solitary, though I made many friends each year in Kilkee, most of whom were press ganged into pitch and putt challenges at the West End. I even played a few times on the pitch and putt course at the Golf Club at the East End of the town, but the attraction of the West End was undoubtedly Bernie and Maureen.

Before long, there was a cheery greeting of "Hiya, John! Gonna beat the record today?" Sometimes my mother would come along and chat to the couple while I hacked my way around the 18 holes, constantly distracted by that view up the coast, over the Duggerna Reef, past George's Head and as far as the Aran islands on a clear day. The sun, the sea, the coastal air and the personal challenge of the 'record', all combined to make it a kind of heaven for that teenager.

There was an attractiveness about the Haughs – an easy going approach which I suspect may have developed from their time in the USA. Kilkee was a faraway place in those days and had a pace of life removed from the mid Sixties hype and hustle elsewhere – so the modern clothes and slight American twang of Bernie and Maureen made them stand out a little, I suppose.

Every year, when we returned to Kilkee, I would go down to the West End, and Maureen would greet me with: "Hiya, John, nice to see you back – how's your mother getting on?" Bernie, it seemed, remained working in America for the summer, but Maureen's welcome never faltered.

The friendly welcome became as important as the pitch and putt, if I'm honest, and, as the years went by, the chat lengthened and the 'record' became less important. I was always amazed that she remembered me – out of the thousands of visitors who must have played the course, and I always looked forward to what became my 'welcome back' to the town.

When I started visiting 'out of season', the pitch and putt would be closed, but, when Maureen knew I was in town, she would leave a couple of clubs and balls in the front porch of "Dunearn" where she lived in the West End, and I would pick them up and drop them off – "no charge". Sometimes, if she was around, there would be an invite in for a cup of tea and a chat about the passing years.

I last met Maureen in 1991.

Having won an award at Listowel Writers' Week, I escaped the festivities for a day and headed for the Killimer ferry and thence to Kilkee. It was my first visit in a while, and I was both excited and nervous. I invest a lot of love in the town, but places – and people – change, and I was not sure what I would find when I turned down the familiar O'Curry St.

There were changes, of course – some I had known about, and others which were a surprise – but Kilkee has always been more than just buildings, and there was a pleasing continuity about the scene.

I parked by the Hydro – by then "Old Moore's Apartments", and walked along the road towards the West End, shadowing that first ever walk in Kilkee. I took in the various changes – and the parts that had stayed the same, and then, with a little trepidation, turned the corner by 'The Dickie Harris house" and looked down the hill.

Nothing seemed to have changed – but there was no guarantee that Maureen would still be behind the counter, or, if she was, that she would remember me after all this time. It felt like an important moment – daft as that may sound – and I did consider walking on to the Diamond Rocks without stopping.

However, as brave as I had been at 14, I pushed at the door and entered a shop which was basically unchanged since 1966.

Behind the counter was Maureen. She looked up and said. "Good afternoon!" When I replied, she said, with no surprise at all, "Well, John – we haven't seen you for a while – how is your mother doing?"

I don't have the words to describe the reaction that generated. On one hand, it was a retailer recognising a good customer from former years, there may be dozens of people to whom Maureen showed such kindness and attention, on the other hand, it was a link with my childhood in a place which had brought me so much joy.

Before I could get too emotional, she said – and I swear the American accent had become more noticeable – "We had a guy in a couple of weeks ago used to come round here with you and your mother back in the sixties – can't remember his name…." It was the perfect introduction to a conversation in which we reminisced and she learned about what I had been doing – and the fact that I had a son and wife who had already visited Kilkee.

I bought a bar of chocolate, for old times sake, and headed off to the Diamond Rocks. As I closed the door she said: "See ya!"

Thanks to the internet, it has been possible to keep up to date with at least some Kilkee news without actually visiting. I saw at some point that Maureen seemed to have moved a couple of houses along from "Dunearn" to "Duggerna" and realised, as time passed, it was unlikely that she would still be running the pitch and putt.

I paid a flying visit to the town about four or five years ago. I knew from my online news that the "Diamond Rocks' Café had been constructed at the West End, as had the statue of Dickie Harris in racquets pose, so I had no false illusions of what I would find as I drove down to the end of the road. A "danger" sign in Polish served to illustrate the changes through the years – but I was glad that Kilkee seems to prosper thanks to the townspeople's hard work. The café attracts rave reviews and I occasionally treated myself to a look at the view from their webcam – a view that remains familiar.

The business is still in the family – though Kilkee has so many Haughs you would be hard put to work out relationships!

I couldn't call Maureen a friend. In reality we knew very little about each other – but what a legacy, to be a casual acquaintance and to make such an impact on a stranger's life; to be a kind of totem for the effect of humanity, kindness, and friendliness. How many more people, I wonder, were affected so positively by that lovely woman in the West End?

Whatever the reality on the road to the Diamond Rocks, I think she will always be there, waiting with that friendly welcome, that recognition which said, somehow, that you mattered.

It would be nice to think that she has encountered my mother in that part of Heaven which isn't Kilkee, and I hope they are having a good catch up.

From my earliest days in Kilkee, our pub of choice was Egan's, just down from the Arcadia in O'Curry St. It was another of those associations which came about through my mother who formed a friendship with Mrs Egan – again on the grounds of them both being widows.

By the time I was 16 one of our weekly highlights was a singing session in the pub's 'middle bar' which was run by another Kilkee character – Ted Kavanagh.

The 'urban rumour' – which I was never able to confirm or disprove – was that Ted – a big, friendly man, with the look of John Goodman playing Fred Flintstone – had benefited from a sizeable win on the Sweepstakes Lottery. With his winnings, he had set up his auctioneer's business on O'Curry St and bought a Hammond organ.

Once a week, he would base himself in Egan's and play an eclectic mix of classics, favourites, country, and folk tunes on the keyboard – happy if folk sang along, but betraying no reaction if they failed to do so. Much like the Hydro lounge, there seemed to be a tipping point where someone would offer to sing, and Ted would either play along or let the singer proceed unaccompanied. Young folk would bring in guitars and give it a belt on the old rebel songs, and older folk would recall long ago hits from John Count McCormick or Fr Sydney McEwan.

The lounge was small and these sessions had an intimate feel to them – while you might be a little intimidated by the size and quality of the offerings in the Hydro, here it felt like anyone could join in, and this was facilitated by Ted's deadpan performance – broken only occasionally by a shout of "Go on there, missus!" or "Fair play yerself!"

The premises ran through from O'Curry St to the Strandline and overlooking the bay was Egan's "Sun Haven Bar". This mostly operated as a morning café for restorative coffees – either sitting in the garden, or indoors, sheltered from the breeze, gazing out through the panoramic window, waiting for John Egan to serve us with coffee and biscuits as we discussed last night and the day ahead.

In the sixties I think there were thirty eight pubs in the town, but Egan's was the place we got to know best, and therefore, as I got older, the bar I was most likely to visit.

Apart from Mrs Egan, we got to know her son, John, who would sometimes help out around the bar, but one of my favourite folk in Kilkee for a time was their barman, Raymond Russell.

Because, as a student, my later visits tended to be at Easter or in September – folk like Ray were not busy and had more time to chat. For a visitor, in a place they love, there is little better than being welcomed into a comfortable bar by name. Ray was friendly and chatty, poured a great pint, and made the best Irish Coffee I have ever tasted –which he always served in a plain coffee cup and saucer – none of the "special glass" patter! He also taught me a fair bit of Irish, and generally made myself and my friends feel welcome in Egan's, whenever we dropped in.

However, year round barman in Kilkee is not an occupation to make your fortune, and he started to talk about going to Cork to qualify as a radio operator in the merchant navy. As inevitably happens, when he left Egan's, we lost contact. The last news I heard of him, back in the seventies, was that he was working as manager of a club in Limerick – the Pink Elephant or the Purple Pussycat or some such. He was a nice guy – one of many who contributed to my love of Kilkee.

I would not want to give the impression of being a hardened drinker, but another pal I had for a while was Gerry Hennessey from Kilrush. He had worked as a barman at the Hydro and then at the Marine. It was good to meet him each year and we sometimes would go out for a pint and a chat when he was off duty.

Many years later, in the nineties, I was crossing the Shannon from Tarbert to Killimer on the ferry when I realised it was Gerry who was taking the fares. Again, as with P.J. King, in an ideal world I would have jumped out of the car and identified myself, but he was busy and I had the family with me and in the end I satisfied myself with being content to know he was still well and working and in the locality.

These were all local folk who I knew and who knew me – but, as is the case in any small town, there were more than a few people who were well known characters whom I knew but who would not have known who I was.

Sometimes they just flitted in and out of sight: Timmy McInerney for me was the man who kept the flower beds in such grand condition at the Hydro – it would be many years later that I would discover his great service to Kilkee as Town Clerk for so many decades.

Tom Haugh was familiar to me as the sacristan at the church and by the advert for his barber's business outside the low cottage in Chapel St. I learned later he had promoted hurling in the town, and on the strand, for a long time. He had a fierce look about him and cropped hair and the local lads would suggest you would get scalped if you patronised his business, but it lasted for over fifty years, so he can't have been that bad at the haircutting!

In the church itself were Fr, later Canon, Kenny and, as curate, another great GAA man, Fr Culligan. There is a priest of that name now at Carrigaholt, and I would like it think it is the same man. The curate was more familiar to me, I suppose, as his house in Albert Place was just next to the Hydro, so I would see him about a bit. I will write about the church later, but such was its size and the crowds that attended Mass each Summer that Canon Kenny was a distant figure to me, mostly familiar through the booming and echoing public address system which the church possessed – sometimes it felt like we were listening to the word of God, in actuality, rather than merely theologically!

The last time I saw the Parish Priest, Fr Kenny, was one Summer in late August when P.J. King was driving us off to Shannon at the end of our stay. He would always drive slowly along the Strandline so we could have a last look at the bay, and, as we turned up the hill between Nolan's and the Stella Maris, I looked round for a farewell glimpse of the strand. There on the beach, a coat over his cassock, breviary in hand and his dog running around him, was Canon Kenny.

It has formed an iconic image for me ever since, and, I suppose, Canon Kenny was a typical example of the old style Parish priest in rural Ireland: gruff and authoritarian but with a commitment to his flock – for better or worse.

Though Egan's tended to be our pub of choice through the years, we did visit other bars and hotels. Nobody who knew Kilkee in those days would be unaware of the Scott brothers and their place on O'Curry St. They ran an establishment which was as iconically out of date as the ship on the faded poster for transatlantic voyages which was the centrepiece of their front window. To go into Scotts was to step back in time, as they stood behind the bar, identically dressed in their white shirts, slowly polishing the glasses and dispensing local news and gossip.

That they were within hailing distance of another great old Kilkee institution – Peggy Starr's Hairdresser's and Off License - used to fuel many a soap operatic fancy about romance and unification of bar and hairdressers.

My mother would go to Peggy Starr's to have her hair styled when we were in Kilkee, and got friendly with Peggy. She never failed to come away with some piece of news about the town or well known visitors. For years I was enthralled by the name: "Peggy Starr". I imagined she had chosen in it in the early sixties, in an era when pop stars had names like Marty Wilde and Billy Fury, to add some glamour to O'Curry St. It was only when she died in 2014 that I discovered her actual name had been, in fact: Margaret Starr! Another assumption ruined!

There were folk who were obvious and well known to all visitors: the guy who ran the amusements in Church Rd – dodgem cars and a shooting gallery – stood out with his waistcoat, stetson, and eye patch, while Scotsman, Wally Maxwell, who ran the slot machines at the bottom of O'Curry St by the roundabout, was hard to miss, with his red cheeks, unfeasibly auburn wig, and larger than life personality.

A group of lads could be spotted most days, standing discussing the world and having a smoke by the low wall in front of the old school house with its "Bingo" adverts, at the corner of Marine Parade and Church Rd. Eugene Costello, brother of Cyril, our waiter friend in the Hydro, and sometimes a porter in the hotel as well, was one of them

The folk who served us in the various shops year by year became familiar: in The Cherry Tree bakery, Collins Medical Hall, Williams Hardware and Pharmacy, Murphy's Café by the Vic, the West End Stores, Buckley's, (including their old black dog, who loved dozing on the pavement outside the shop in the sun), The Irish House, Moloney's clothing store, the ice cream machine at the Arcadia, and in Haugh's Central Stores – where hamburgers were always available after the Hydro dance. I remember particularly enjoying a burger one night and then realising with a start that, as it was after midnight, it was Friday, and I really should not have been eating meat. That was maybe as wild as I got in Kilkee!

Part of our entertainment was provided by the telephone exchange – which was actually a small room in the modest post office, which at the time was situated in Circular Rd opposite Williams. When I first arrived in Kilkee, the services could be intermittent. There were occasional power cuts, the water often ran brown, and to make a phone call you wound a handle to contact the operator. She sat at the switchboard and pulled the plugs in and out – or informed you that the person you were calling had gone to Ennis and wouldn't be back till later! The exchange had a window which looked out on to the road, and, if they had forgotten to pull down the venetian blind, it was possible for us to stand with our noses pressed against the glass, making faces and trying to distract the poor operator as she flicked the switches and pulled the plugs which would connect Kilkee to the outside world.

Various publicans and hoteliers, like Michael Martin and Tom Kett, would be the stuff of legend: most visitors knew who they were without ever having met them. Stories would circulate without there being any way of ascertaining whether they were true, exaggerated, or totally fabricated – the stuff of chatter in small town life. Often they would involve the clergy or the Guards and their interaction with townsfolk.

One such involved Tom Kett, after he was seen around town with his foot in a plaster cast. As it was told, Tom had been involved in a lock in after hours, either in his own bar or in another establishment. Either way, there was a new Sergeant at the Barracks, who seemed immune to the need of Kilkee's licensed premises to avail themselves of all the opportunities available for their Summer income. He had taken to knocking on the doors of buildings where curtains were tightly drawn and lights well masked after hours.

So, according to the tale, in fear of the implications for his licence, if caught, Tom had left through the back door as the Sergeant had rapped on the front door, and a chase through the town had ensued. This had ended when Tom burst into the lounge of the Victoria Hotel, jumped over the bar, landed awkwardly, and broke his ankle.

I have no idea of the veracity of the tale – but it's a good one, and it was certainly popular currency in Kilkee one Summer!

It may be that, in a resort where, traditionally, many holidaymakers returned year after year, familiarity with local figures played a part in making them feel welcome, relaxed, and, paradoxically, "at home." For those of us who returned time and again there was certainly an element of the "Kilkee soap opera" as we came back annually to discover who had stayed, who had left, and what changes had been made.

Through all of that, however, there was one constant, one certainty, and that was Manuel Di Lucia.

A lot of people have committed to hard work all through their lives to help Kilkee survive and hopefully prosper – some I have mentioned here, some came on to the stage after my time in the town, or served on the council, or in other ways that made them less obvious to the visiting community, but there is no doubting Manuel's influence on Kilkee these past fifty years or more.

Anybody who spent any amount of time in the town would have recognised the name and the man. He worked to develop sub aqua exploring and diving in the town, and boating and fishing also benefited. The facilities for visitors and the marine based attractions were developed, as were rescue facilities with the work of many local folk. Many tourists came from the Low Countries and Scandinavia who would not have heard of Kilkee were it not for the promotion of the clear water diving opportunities and the building up of a support infrastructure in the town. He also served as Town Mayor.

I remember when it was decided to launch a Kilkee Family Festival Week in the late 60s. It was in the third week of August and its aim was to extend the season. The Strand Races were re-started, there was a fancy dress parade, events in many of the pubs and hotels, and a grand gala dance to end the week in the Hydro Ballroom. Manuel kindly asked my mother if she would be one of the judges for the parade, a request with which she was delighted, and showed a shrewd understanding of promotional activities on the part of Manuel. He was reaching out to a regular visitor, which made her feel welcomed into the community, and sending a message about Kilkee hospitality.

The Festival also featured the redoubtable Agnes O'Connell, with her "London Irish Girl Pipers" – and an impressive sight they made marching along the Strandline in their colourful uniforms, the pipes skirling and Agnes leading the way, resplendent in her pillar box red jacket, with her tam o' shanter worn at a jaunty angle. Manuel introduced her to my mother, and the pair, predictably, got on famously.

The racquets competitions, and the town's Richard Harris connections as a tourist attraction also received Manuel's attention, and, of course, in the early days, his Savoy Café in O'Curry St would be the fast food, late night, centre for all of us, and often other members of the family, such as his brother, Christy, would be serving.

Later, in the 80s, I remember a meal on a glorious summer evening in the seafood restaurant he opened in his lovely house at Corbally, with its stunning views down the coast past Moore Bay. He was an attentive host, a fine cook, and knew how to make a simple meal special. Happy days indeed!

One name I knew in the town was all but invisible as a person, and, in fact, it was only in the past year that I have discovered that he actually existed at all.

On O'Curry St, next to Collins Medical Hall, there was a gap site. In the late 60s a wooden hut, painted a dull red, appeared on the pavement in front of the empty space. In big red letters a sign announced: "Frank Snaps" and in the windows of the hut were pinned black and white contact sheets with hundreds of photographs.

It was, of course, a good marketing title – the snaps were indeed 'frank', but they were also taken by "Frank" – or his acolytes. The company was a direct descendant of the 'street photographers' of the 1940s and 50s.

In those days, only a minority of families would have a camera, and, for those who possessed such a thing, the setting up of camera and subject to get a decent print was often more trouble than it was worth, especially when the spool had to be finished and then sent away or taken into a chemists for development.

As a result, there existed a body of men who operated rather like the paparazzi, but focusing on ordinary folk rather than celebrities. They would patrol seaside promenades and tourist spots, jump out with their camera and take a candid shot of a couple walking along, and then try and sell them the result. Most folk of my generation will have at home at least one photograph of their parents or grandparents out for a stroll along the prom when they were surprised by such a cameraman.

It turns out that "Frank Snaps" was run by Limerick man, Frank Goggin, and he had, for years, been taking pictures in Ballybunion and Lahinch and Limerick city and such places. By the sixties, he was operating mainly in ballrooms – like the Stella or the Jetland in Limerick, or the Hydro in Kilkee.

For the summer season he often employed students and they would circle the floor in the dance hall, snap pictures of close dancing couples, and then press a ticket into your hand. I remember in Kilkee, the tickets were dark pink with serrated edges and you had to tear around the edges to unfold them. Inside would be a number and an invitation to contact either Frank's studios in Limerick or the kiosk in O'Curry St the next day. There, using your number, you could view a miniature, black and white, print of your photograph, and if it pleased you, it could be ordered full sized for around two shillings, (or ten cents now) – about the price of a pint in those days, and either sent to your home or picked up from the kiosk in a couple of days.

In these days of camera phones and Instagram, the idea of "sending a film away" to be developed, or even having to wait to see what a picture looked like, must seem bizarre, but it certainly gave Frank a lifelong career, and somewhere in an attic there may be thousands of black and white pictures of couples dancing their youth away in long closed down ballrooms – a real social history source.

I do not know what percentage of subjects actually bought a print, or even checked them out, but while it was in Kilkee, the kiosk was a great focal point for visitors and locals alike, trying to spot who had been at the Hydro and with whom they had been dancing. I imagine there must have been the odd scandal or cause for explanation identified, and we should maybe think of it as an early, if static, version of Facebook!

Sometimes there were people who featured in our holidays and I only fully realised who they were years later. This was true to an extent of Hilda O'Malley, Gus Weldon and Dermot Harris in the Hydro, but also of some guests later on in the Marine.

As I said, the Marine tended to have an, older clientele than the Hydro and I don't suppose we took too much notice of some of the elderly people who were around. Nevertheless, there was a friendly and relaxed atmosphere about the place and we would often have a wee chat in the Lounge or Dining Room if our paths crossed.

One elderly man who visited with, I believe, his sister and niece, was a Mr Redmond. He must have been in his late seventies when we stayed at the Marine, but, as was the case with his generation, was always dressed impeccably, with jacket, shirt and tie and flannels. Along with his companions, he would always stop and chat about our day when our paths crossed, and soon he became "Owen" instead of "Mr Redmond".

Sometime later I came to discover that "Owen Redmond" had been Secretary to the Department of Finance in the mid 1950s, and, as predecessor to T.K. Whittaker, had laid a lot of the groundwork for Ireland's economic progress as an independent State under Taoisigh Costello and Lemass. There was no hint of that about his demeanour when we knew him.

Another venerable Marine resident was a Mr Mulcahy. He seemed older than Owen Redmond, and was accompanied by his wife. He was very smartly turned out at all times, I can still remember the shine on his brown shoes, always worn with smart trousers and a tweed jacket. Though he was quite withdrawn and non-communicative, his wife was very pleasant and would chat away at length if we found ourselves in the lounge or dining room at the same time.

I discovered a few years later that "Mr Mulcahy" was Richard Mulcahy, who had fought in Easter Week, become Chief of Staff of the IRA and then the Free State Army, leader of Fine Gael, and holder of many cabinet posts, including Minister for Education. There had been little or no interaction between us, but it was still fascinating to know that we had been in the company of such a seminal figure in twentieth century Irish history – and, of course, as time goes by, that "human connection" assumes even more significance. In retrospect, it is easy to suggest that there was a military bearing about him, but, being honest, at the time, he just seemed to be a frail old gentleman.

It turned out, though, that his wife, at least from my point of view, carried an even more fascinating story.

With the 2016 centennial commemoration of the Easter Rising, more information has become available – or at least received a higher profile. The role of women, and tales of the Leaders' family lives, have come more to the fore. Often, it has been the family moments, revealing the "Leaders" as humans rather than icons, which have been most poignant.

We are all aware of the marriage of Grace Gifford and Joseph Plunkett in the Kilmainham Jail Chapel shortly before his execution, Connolly's last meeting with his wife and daughter, and the various hopes expressed for their children in the Leaders' last letters. Particularly, affecting is the description of Tomás MacDonagh's baby daughter waking from her sleep to hug him, as he kissed her goodbye for the last time before leaving to take part in the Rising.

However, given my family's connections to Leitrim, Seán MacDiarmada has always been a particular hero of mine. Not only do we share north Leitrim origins, but his first job was as a gardener in Edinburgh, my birthplace. Re-reading his final letters shortly before Easter this year, I came upon his reference to Min Ryan "who, in all probability, would have been my wife, had I lived." She had been a courier in the GPO during Easter Week. The article then pointed out that she had gone on to marry Richard Mulcahy. The realisation that I had met and talked with the woman who had last been with MacDiarmada only forty five minutes before his execution was moving, to say the least. It was typical of Kilkee, I thought, that an elderly couple in a hotel lounge would turn out to be so intricately linked to the foundation of the State.

As I have commented about other people I met in the town, my ignorance of their significance, at the time, is not a regret. I was a teenager, and a shy one at that. I cannot imagine how I would have reacted had I known of their background. It is hard to envisage my sitting next to Owen Redmond in the lounge and saying: "So, Owen, how was it you set the Irish economy rolling?" Similarly, an opening gambit in the dining room of "Seán MacDiarmada, Mrs Mulcahy – what was he really like?" would never really have been feasible!

That a small and rather remote town could lead to such encounters reflects part of Kilkee's charm and attraction I suppose. It also occurs to me as I write that, through this, I became involved in the kind of irony which perhaps can only be found in a small country in the aftermath of internecine strife.

One of our favourite songs in Egan's Lounge was the fervent Republican ballad: "Take it down from the Mast." Little did I know that I would leave Egan's to return to the Marine, and wish a gentle good night to the old man in the lounge who, as head of the Free State forces, was largely responsible for much of the bitterness in the song I had just been singing.

It was not always about history. Years later, at a concert by the Dublin City Ramblers, in Tom Kett's Lounge, I got friendly with a guy sitting next to us. We had a grand session, but it was only well into the evening that I realised he was Eoin Hand, and was, at the time, the Republic's soccer manager. He was not too popular at the time, so maybe he needed a friend!

Of course, there were many other characters around the town who were familiar to all – like Maggie who sold winkles from a barrow on the Strandline just down from the Stella Maris, and others who had no names but were recognised each year. People tended to return to Kilkee for the same weeks each year, so there was a familiarity about the visitors as well as the residents – you would see the same cars parked outside the same lodges each August, familiar towels hanging from the windows to dry, the swimmers, the walkers, the golfers – all became familiar, and added to the comfort of being in Kilkee on holiday. Again.

Later, I will examine why we go on holiday, what we expect, and how that has changed over the years. However, when I look back on my early years of visiting Kilkee – as well as the place, it was the people who made me long to get there each August – the ones I could say I knew, and the ones who only played a part in the background. They were, I suppose, the dressing on the set, the added constituent which made a beautiful place extra special.

It is a comparison which I have made time and again through the decades: Kilkee was, in a sense, a soap opera into which I could dip for a few weeks every year. The characters were often in my mind when I was not there, memories of things that had happened came back to me often, and, as I lived my "real" life in another country – originally England, and then Scotland – thoughts of what had happened, and what might be happening, around Moore Bay often accompanied my every day activities.

Unconsciously, the people – residents and visitors alike – played their parts in that comforting distraction – but then, so did many places in the town and around about. It was knowing it was all there, waiting for my return, that added to the magic!

THERE ARE PLACES IN MY PAST……

I can imagine that any folk under forty who might be reading this memoir must be a little puzzled.

The attraction of the dancehall and the pub and hotel sessions translates down through the years - even if transformed into "clubbing" and "karaoke". However, the youngsters must be wondering what else we did to fill our time back in the sixties in Kilkee, given the furious pace at which smartphone-connected teenagers live their lives these days.

I think, the answer to their mystification explains part of Kilkee's attraction at that time. In the sixties, amusement for young people was very often self provided. Record players and radios were popular but obviously lacked the mobility that today's music providers possess. Coffee shops as we know them today were unheard of, and though teenagers were big news, the rampant manipulation of their spending power was not yet finely tuned.

For many of us, at home, as well as on holiday, meeting up and "wandering about town" was our main leisure activity. It sounds lame to modern ears, I am sure, but with no other choice, it tended to be what we did. If we were lucky we might have a local record store where we could all pile into a sound booth and listen to the latest records – till the owner ascertained that we were unlikely to buy anything. In the mid sixties, "shopping" was not considered a pastime, and, without mobile phones, even the act of meeting up with your pals could take some arranging.

What Kilkee provided for holiday makers – especially from outwith Ireland – was an interesting collection of streets, walks, shops, houses and alleyways, which could be explored day after day and would always turn up something interesting. In addition, there was a stronger than even chance that you would bump into folk who you knew whenever you wondered about the place.

I don't think I ever saw a detailed map of Kilkee until around twenty years after my first visit. Few of the streets had name signs and, as I have mentioned, directions tended to be by references to hotels, pubs, or shops. We had never heard of Allender's Field – to us it would be the slope in front of the burnt out pink lodge, which we were unaware was in Mount Charles Terrace; Erin St was "down the side of the Stella Maris" and Grattan St was "at the back of the Square". When we meandered down the lane at the side of the post office and found ourselves in O'Curry St, we didn't know it was called Post Office Lane and always felt like we might be trespassing. Whilst we might have heard of the Strandline, Marine Parade and McDonnell Terrace were not familiar names to us.

Generally we talked of the West End, George's Head, O'Curry St and the Dunlicky Rd – but to wander round the town was a real treat for us.

In the East End, with its 'model estate layout', the roads were wide, the houses low and surprisingly individual – doors, window decorations, stonework, colour and adornment all told stories of those who lived there; over it all hung a marvellously different, stirring and redolent aroma of turf smoke from the fires.

At the West End, there was a huge variety of architecture from original Victorian to relatively modern, and various designs to allow the buildings cling on to the rocky slopes above the shoreline. Right around the strandline the names and styles of lodges, guest houses, private homes and holiday properties would fascinate - as would the various signs of habitation: inflatable dinghies, flapping bathing towels, beach toys, canoes, bicycles, telescopes, model ships, family dogs, and, parked outside, the distinctive number plates of cars from many counties.

As I have said, some of these signs became familiar. You might recognise that the same family had returned for another year without knowing anything about them, their name, or even where they were from – you just recognised the same signs of their presence that you had seen last year and the year before.

So we wandered round town, became comfortable with all the shops – whether or not we patronised them, associated familiar faces with the same bars, went for the paper from the Irish House at 6pm every day, bought ice cream from outside the Arcadia, or chocolate from Haugh's Central Stores, gazed at the assembled collection of seaside paraphernalia in Buckley's window, smelled the somehow exciting combination of hardware, paraffin, and medical supplies in John Williams' on the Circular Rd – and viewed the postcards on display outside. We might go into Maguire's the Chemists on O'Curry St near the cinema and sort through the two racks of 45rpm records – the only outlet for records in the town; I remember buying the Carousel Showband's single "Holiday Romance" from there – how appropriate! The folk playing croquet in front of Clar Elagh might attract our attention, or a horse galloping on the strand; it was always fun to peer through the window of the Fire Station at the open cab of the 1930 Merryweather fire engine and to scramble down the lane at the side on to the Strandline.

Occasionally we would wander around Merton Square, wondering about the stories behind the once grand houses, visiting the Hydro staff in their lodgings next to the Olympia Hall.

Along the West End, our attention was spread between the various lodges and guest houses and the rocks below the wall and the bay and the reef out beyond. "Dickie Harris's House" was always an object of interest, and I guess we always half hoped he would emerge, but we didn't know that when he was in Kilkee he generally stayed at the Hydro, and, according to Manuel, who looked after the house for him, only ever spent one night in the place.

Newfoundout, with its steps and diving board attached to the steep rocks always took the eye, though I was never remotely interested in bathing there. I do remember one time I was in Kilkee alone, sitting on the bench there for the better part of a day, engrossed in a book, punctuating my reading with long looks across the bay and out beyond the Duggerna Reef – a perfect way to spend a few hours.

Similarly, I was never tempted to swim at the Pollock Holes – indeed, much preferring to be by the sea rather than in it, I don't suppose I've been in the sea at Kilkee more than a dozen times over the years. However, to scramble across the reef, leaping from rock to rock, hearing the pop of the seaweed beneath your feet, hoping the darkness on the rock on to which you jumped was not slime, heart moving moments of losing your balance, and quiet moments of lying down, looking deep into clear pools, where marine plants gently waved and unknowable sea creatures scuttled about – all of this brought a kind of magic to the day. Even fifty yards from the shore, it felt like another world, and the salt on your lips and the spray on your face confirmed that you were part of it.

I have already written of Haugh's Pitch and Putt – which was much more than just an opportunity to play a reduced version of golf. The original shed in which they had their shop was full of atmosphere, and often, in the early days, had included the presence of the older generation – generally referred to as "Old Man" or "Pa" Haugh. The urban rumour department had Dickie Harris as a regular visitor when he was in town, usually accompanied by gangs of youngsters. He would ask the old man for something from the top shelf and then, when his back was turned, would show the kids how they could lift handfuls of chocolate bars from the counter. To be fair, the legend also had it that he would later return to pay for the sweets and to buy bottles of lemonade which he would distribute to the youngsters on the strand. Whether these tales were true or not, they added to the appeal of the place.

Aside from the welcome you would receive from Maureen and Bernie, it was a straightforward fact that the position of the pitch and putt course was magnificent. The views were up the coast towards the Aran islands and across the bay and to George's Head, and behind you Lookout Hill raised up majestically, the sheep shelter at the bottom of its slope, always white against the shades of green. It was one of the locations in Kilkee where it could feel that you were somehow outside of time – the sea breeze, the sun, the ocean blue, the high, clear sky, and the rolling hills around - all combined to freeze frame the moment and elevate the mind. There, enjoying where you were and what you were doing, it was impossible to feel anything but happy.

If the pitch and putt didn't detain you, then the cliff walk would draw you on.

The first distraction was the amphitheatre. To folk who don't know Kilkee that must sound that a grandiloquent name for a natural phenomenon on the cliffs, but there really is not any other description which fits. Only about twenty yards off the walking path, this inlet is truly astonishing when first viewed.

As the name suggests, tiers of rock are arranged round a u-shaped cove, like seats in an arena. The ledges so formed are irregular in shape and thickness and in colour they range from almost black through brownish red to navy blue, flecked with ochre runs of clay. They display the strata of thousands of years quite clearly and I imagine the NUIG archaeology and geomorphology students who have examined this coast must have written many a report on this unique feature.

Like many areas on the west Clare coast around Kilkee, the amphitheatre offers many spots where you can just sit with a book, or your thoughts, and contemplate the greatness of the sea and the power of its waves, while birds fly across your vision like messengers on some unknown errand.

One of its attractions is how differently it appears depending on the height of the tide or the strength of the winds. There are tiny crevices where rock and maritime plants spring up in their surprising pinks and reds and whites. You would not think anything could grow in such an exposed position, especially when you can easily see the thinness of the earth where it does lie over a rocky base.

I'm not sure we noticed too much of this in our youth; we seemed to be constantly on the move. There were always tales of parties and barbecues being held late into the night at the Amphitheatre, marvellous sixties' tales of long haired soulful youths crouched over guitars while a pretty girl with flowing locks and long skirts sang mournfully, like a latterday leanan sidhe, and the dull light of flickering campfire flames brought haunting shadows to the inlet. It is a lovely thought – but I never met anyone who had actually been at one of these events, and I can't say I would have relished wandering about on these cliffs after dark. Like so many other "ancient tales" of Kilkee, perhaps it is best to say it added to the legend, and contributed to the atmosphere.

Inevitably, we would be drawn onwards and upwards.

At the top of the slope in the sixties was a rickety fence and the rumour of a stile, perhaps. The ground here was muddy with clay that had run off the fields and after rain it could be quite tricky to negotiate, though there was a gap through which you could access the cliffs ahead.

However, by the end of the decade, you would have found a breeze block wall with an obvious entry gap and the muddy ground stabilised by light coloured cobbles.

This was one of the more obvious consequences of the decision by Faraway Productions and MGM to spend the best part of a year in Kilkee waiting for a suitable storm to film for their epic, "Ryan's Daughter". I would find these cobbles again – around the schoolhouse which was built in Cill Gobnait near Dún Chaoin in west Kerry, and up on top of Carhoo Mountain where the main street of "Kirrary" is still discernible. There are some iconic pictures of the film crews on the cliffs here and up on Lookout Hill as they struggled to batten down their cameras and lights in the teeth of a wild Atlantic gale, and as I will mention later on, the storm section, which for many was the highlight of the film, features many shots of this area. The second unit director, Charles Friend, who was responsible for the filming around Kilkee and west Clare, did a brilliant job, but received scant recognition from David Lean, who feared he might lose some of his own directorial glory, as the storm scene was so widely praised.

Of course, to those of us who loved Kilkee, it was the scenery, as much as the cinematography, which made those parts of the film so memorable!

Beyond the wall and the hardstanding, the ground was undisturbed, which is either a testimony to MGM's rehabilitation of the area or suggests that the heavy machinery was based down at this level and maybe on the Dunlicky Road. Either way, the path from this point onwards, in those early days, was very basic and crossed at regular intervals by drainage run offs from the fields, which meant you had to watch your footing. In addition, where these channels had widened and crumbled, the cliff edges became dangerous and the walk entailed elements of uncertainty which would probably not be tolerated in these days of enhanced health and safety provision.

Of course, that mattered not to us as we made our way along the cliff tops, chattering, singing, being archetypally youthful without any realisation of the fact. I am not sure that walking was as popular a pastime as it was to later become, and very often we would find ourselves alone on those fields – which only added to the beauty of it all.

We would skirt around Intrinsic Bay – the name of which was unknown to us – and lie flat on the turf to look down from the sheer heights.

Far below, the waves crashed into small caves at the foot of the rocky cliffs, they churned white and cream, dark blue and light blue, turquoise and black. Birds wheeled and flew upwards in the draft of inconsistent gusts of wind, their cries snatched away almost before you could hear them. Beyond was the wide sea, the cliffs of the coast to the north, and sometimes the Aran Islands, almost there in the sea mist. It gave you a feeling of awe, of power, of insignificance and, more than anything, it was an affirmation of the vitality of life. It could make you shout out loud for joy.

Intrinsic Bay, like Edmond Point, reflected an aspect of my early days in Kilkee which, with perspective, is quite important. As in every "love at first sight" relationship, I fell head over heels on first visiting the town without any knowledge which went deeper than the obvious first impressions. My love for the town was none the less genuine, however, and, as would be the case when "instant love" turned into a long term relationship, the more I found out over the years, the more my love deepened and respect increased.

That first morning, as I have described, Edmond Point was, for me, a place to discover marine life, to jump from rock to rock, breathe in the sea air and feel the relaxation of early holiday excitement. It has always been a special part of Kilkee for me, because of that.

However, learning of its name and of how it acquired it, I gained another layer of understanding and reflection when thinking of this rocky place, so close to the sea wall.

Reading accounts of the Edmond's last voyage, it is impossible not to be affected by a feeling of doom, a feeling which seems so out of place in this spot which holidaymakers think of as peaceful and quiet.

While I am making my way, as it were, across the beauty and peace of the cliff top walk, it is maybe a good time to reflect on what happened to both the Edmond and the Intrinsic – even for those who know Kilkee and are well acquainted with the stories. Just as I often paused at both spots to remember those who lost their lives there, maybe in this written account of Kilkee, which, for all my recounting of fabulous moments, I am trying to make realistic, it is as well to remember that the power and beauty of nature, with which Kilkee is so well endowed, comes at a cost.

The Edmond was wrecked at Kilkee on November 19th 1850, having set sail from Limerick and previously called in at Carrigaholt, from where she departed on the 18th of November. She was a nine hundred and eighty ton, three masted sailing vessel, chartered by a Limerick timber merchant so that on outward voyages she took emigrants to a new life in the New World, and returned with a cargo of timber.

Though it had been relatively calm when she left Carrigaholt, the portents were not good. Kilkee and the peninsula had been ravaged by the Famine and there was an air of gloom over the town all through the year, with many empty lodges and few visitors. A visitor had drowned in the West End in August and another person was missing in September – the same month a "sea monster" had been spotted off Bishop's Island.

Thirty miles off the coast, the vessel was caught in a great storm and driven towards the shore. Eventually she was grounded on the Duggerna Reef at the mouth of Moore Bay and then, having been lifted off the rocks by the rising tide, was cast ashore on the point of rocks in the bay below Sykes's House at the West End.

Those staying in Sykes's could hear the groaning of timbers and the shouts of the passengers even above the roaring of the storm, and three coast guards were quickly in the scene. The ship's Master had the presence of mind to cut down the remaining mast so that the rigging fell on to the rocks, forming a bridge for passengers to be helped ashore, despite the howling gale. For a time it must have seemed that, as close to land as they were, the worst of the tragedy might be averted – but the storm worsened even more and the waters rose higher and the ship broke in two.

Ironically, the crew, who had fulfilled their duty by staying on board, were mostly saved, as they were on the poop deck and managed to survive being flung into the sea. The passengers who were aft were trapped when the remnants of the boat turned over and was cast upon the strand, and they were found deceased inside at daylight. The ships carpenter, John Finn, reported as rescuing up to fifteen people on to the rocks at Sykes's, had returned to the hold to secure his carpenter's chest, and perished when the ship was torn apart.

Contemporary reports make grim reading, with tales of bodies being laid out on the grass in front of Marine Parade, debris from the wreck being strewn across the whole extent of the strand, survivors wandering around in confusion and remains being washed up over subsequent weeks. The kindness of people, from Kilkee and beyond, given their own straitened circumstances, was remarkable.

It is difficult now to stop at Edmond Point and understand how so many could perish so close to the normality of a guest house and its garden, especially when you would be hearing the cries of happy children down on the strand, as a contrast to the screams of the shipwrecked who had scrambled towards the rocks - now the haunt of sunbathers.

Recent storms, and the damage they have caused around the sea wall at Kilkee, have been a reminder of the sea's destructive power, even in such a seemingly sheltered spot. Back in the sixties, before we learned the story of the Edmond, we would not have thought it possible.

The final irony is that those on board had set out so recently for what they hoped would be a better life. In the event, out of a crew and passenger list of two hundred and sixteen, ninety eight died that night, including thirty children and ten infants.

One year, my pal, Daragh O'Malley, stayed at Sykes's House. He defied the odds by often climbing up the drainpipe as access to his room after the door was locked – and we thought that was as dangerous as things could get in that part of the West End!

How little we knew.

However, if Edmond Point seems an unlikely spot for a shipwreck, it is all too easy to imagine disaster as we look down on the rocks and churning waters of Intrinisc Bay.

When the local coast guard climbed Lookout Hill on January 30th 1836 he spotted the vessel Intrinsic, both anchors lowered attempting to ride out a violent storm below the cliffs. She was bound for New Orleans out of Liverpool. Inevitably the anchors failed and the ship was hurled against the rocks, apparently not helped by the fact that her hatches appeared, unaccountably, to be open, allowing her to ship water at an unsustainable level.

We have a detailed account of the wreck, written and published in the same year, and therefore, presumably, based on the eye witness reports, as a note in Mary John Knott's "Two Months at Kilkee"

The report of the disaster is in Knott's Victorian style and we should, I expect, allow for a little exaggeration. What is clear is that the ship had no chance of surviving and, though townspeople, raised by the coastguards, lined the cliffs, there was little they could do by way of rescue.

Whilst the death toll from the Edmond had been the biggest single loss of life from an emigrant ship on the west coast, the Instrinsic's wreck, with fourteen losses, involved less of a human tragedy.

However, the wreck, or at least its immediate aftermath, still has its claim to fame, thanks to Charles Deane, an early diver and salvage expert. He had invented a helmet which would let him descend to great depths, and, at the time, had recently been working around the wreck of Henry the Eighth's lost ship, The Mary Rose, in the Solent off the south coast of England. It had been sunk in the sixteenth century, but Deane had managed to locate some of its guns, and his early exploratory work contributed to its eventual raising from the depths a century and a half later in 1982.

Remarkably, shortly after the wreck, he had managed to recover most of the Intrinsic's cargo, from a depth of up to twelve fathoms, and in so doing, blazed a trail for salvage operations under water.

The Intrinsic was never raised from its watery grave, but there is a nice symmetry in the fact that Kilkee's latter day diving guru, Manuel Di Lucia, was part of a team which located and recovered its anchor in 1979. It is, of course, now displayed on a plinth at the east end of the Strandline – a constant reminder of "those at peril on the seas".

Two other ships have sunk in storms near Kilkee but tend to attract less attention as they were not witnessed by the townspeople and their loss only discovered after the event.

Fifty years to the day of the Intrinsic's loss, on January 30th 1886, the "Fulmar", carrying coal from Troon in Scotland, to Limerick, and listing badly in Force Ten gales went down in Farrihy Bay to the north of the town. Her loss was only realised when wreckage washed up on the strand the following day. Of the seventeen on board, the only body recovered was that of the captain, washed ashore on February 4th.

An even more "invisible" shipwreck was that of the Inishtrahull, another coal ship, a steamer, bound from Glasgow to Limerick. When it failed to arrive in Limerick on December 30th 1894, it was assumed it had taken shelter from the storms and was not in a position from which it could telegraph. However, the Kilkee coastguard picked up a section of a ship's bow upon which "Glasgow" was inscribed, and a disaster was feared. On January 8th, the ship's owners confirmed the loss of twenty five on board the vessel.

Naturally, as a seaside town, Kilkee has lived through the years with deaths at sea. When I was on holiday there, one September in the early 70s, two men were drowned in the bay, barely one hundred yards from the pier. It was a moment of huge impact for me, to be part of a community struck by such sudden tragedy. The place was not in holiday mode, and I was probably one of the few visitors around to witness the disaster. I tried not to intrude, but inevitably my view of Kilkee and its people was thereafter tinged with more reality and understanding, as a progression from my initial starry eyed awe.

These days, in a rather macabre reflection of the changes in Kilkee's tourist industry, many maritime deaths occur amongst visitors, and members of the "new Irish" immigrant community from Europe, who are perhaps unused to the power of the Atlantic along the western cliffs.

The one thing which remains unchanged, however, is the concern shown by local people when tragedy strikes and their outstanding commitment to rescue services in all their guises.

Intrinsic Bay, then, whether through its history, or through the height of its cliffs and the roar of its waves far below, always brings a pause for thought, a moment to reflect on our position in all of this. I always think it would be a good illustration of the biblical phrase: "How great thou art!"

From the almost overwhelming seascape we carry on to something a little more prosaic which is yet another of Kilkee's urban myths, or at least it has always been for me.

As the path curves to the left and upwards towards the heights of Lookout Hill, there is a small white-washed construction which is known as the "sheep shelter". At least, I thought it was, though, as I am writing this, it occurs to me that I have never heard anyone else refer to the building as such. Not so much an "urban myth" then, as a misconception based on my fourteen year old's ignorance back in 1966.

On sober reflection, there is no reason why this would actually be a shelter for sheep. It is small, with a narrow doorway, a bench seat along the interior wall, and porthole type windows to give a view. None of this seems particularly angled towards the sheltering of our woolly friends, especially when the surrounding fields always seemed to be populated by cows.

To be fair, there was very often scatological evidence of various animals within the hut, and this is what may have given rise to my mistake.

No matter, I like the surreal thought of sheep scanning lowering skies over the Atlantic and thinking: "Uh-oh – looks like rain. Better get into the shelter, not much room in there!" – followed by a mad dash to be first through the narrow entrance, and ending with various bits of sheep sticking out through the windows.

Must be the effect of the sea air......

More important than the usage of this building, however, is the fact that it marks the point where the cliff path gives you the choice of Lookout Hill or the Diamond Rocks.

In those days, the steps that led down on to the Diamond Rocks, were rough and ready and soon turned into a rocky path, covered in stones and clay. There was a signpost back in the West End, on the front down from Merton Square, pointing westward to The Diamond Rocks/Na Seod Carraigeacha – but it was very understated and would not have been much help in actually finding them. My memory is that few people went there in the sixties and, certainly, we felt disappointed if we had to share our time there with strangers.

The Diamond Rocks defy description in words.

As you reach the bottom of the rocky steps and turn to the west, you are faced with an amazing scene. On your left, the cliffs raise up maybe twenty feet and are crumbling – a mix of brown earth, blue grey slate coloured rock fragments, sharp edged and in horizontal lines, and the odd maritime plant clinging on.

Beneath your feet the red, brown, marled rock has the smoothness of the ages, with indentations, bewildering shapes, and small pools of water catching the eye.

To the right is a puffing hole, the rocks shining with fallen seawater and, depending on the state of the tide, sudden spurts of spray going high into the air above you.

Ahead of you, slabs and ledges of rock slope away and down to sea level, forming platforms, seats, tables and gullies - every sort of space to sit and wait and watch as nature performs all around.

The dominant rock is sandstone and limestone – reflections of tectonic movement and the shifting of mud and clay millions of years ago – but shales and schist feature too – the schist reported to shine in the sunlight, making the rocks look like "Diamonds" from out at sea.

It does not make for easy walking. The slope is more or less continuous, excepting where rock slippage has left ledges, shelves, and crannies. The rock itself can be treacherously smooth and often deposits of slime are invisible in the bright sunlight, which sometimes turns the pools into mirrors, and at other times make them hidden – till you step in one.

Then there are the limpets, and other signs of sea life: the seaweed, dark blue, brown, black, slippery when wet, popping like bubble wrap when dry, always ready to confuse - whether you are sensibly shod or barefooted.

Because of the formations of the Diamond Rocks, their main attraction is the privacy they offer. People walking on the clifftop need to look out over the very edge to see over the Rocks, and, when you are on the rocks, the different levels and ledges make it easy to find a spot where you are not overlooked at all – even by other people on the Rocks themselves.

It means you can find a spot, settle comfortably, lie with your back supported by the rocks, and contemplate what is around you – free from any interruptions or distractions. You can also choose the level at which you rest – so that, depending on the tides, you can be sitting on rocks at sea level, which are being covered by the incoming waters which surround you, or you can remain aloof and higher, and watch the actions of the waves over many rocks and ledges below.

Depending on your angle, you may have the wide Atlantic ahead – stretching in a vastness of movement which acts almost hypnotically to bring tranquillity, or you may look to the south west – to one of the greatest views I have ever seen anywhere.

Ahead of you is Bishop's island, with Bird Rock to its left. Below you the rocks ease their way down to sea level, by steps and shelves and slopes and mini cliffs, a conglomeration of shapes, but somehow possessing a uniformity: bits of shells, shallow shinings of water and deeper pools containing coral, and seaweed, and plants of impossibly technicoloured hues. Shells of limpets lie attached to the rocks, some seeming almost ingrained in the sandstone itself.

At sea level, the rocks are at different heights, of different shapes, and surrounding hundreds of tiny coves and bays – some no bigger than your hand, others wide enough and deep enough to drown a man.

The tide is relentless in its activity, the waves approach from all angles, find their way with practised ease and then retreat languidly as if the effort of covering the rocks is too much to continue. There is every sound from lap to splash, and foam, which is white, cream, or brown, often trapped in cracks or inlets, waiting to be freed by the next inundation.

The movement, the noise, the variety, and the timelessness of the scene takes your mind – you can lose hours here: sitting, watching, listening, and waiting for some unpredictable signal to urge you to move.

In the distance, Bishop's Island, as it has for centuries, looms up out of the sea and into your imagination. The remains of Senan's Oratory are clear to see, the tales of sheep rearing and monastic routines are well known. The only unfathomable element is the understanding of how men and sheep climbed the sheer cliffs and existed on the sloping meadow atop the rock. It must have been a teasing place for a hermit: so separate from the land, but so close to humanity.

The comprehensible part is the knowledge that, living in the midst of this scenery, with sea, and cliffs, and birds, meditation on the good things of God's earth cannot have been difficult. But still, each time you look upon that island, the mind reaches back over a thousand years, and wants to know the story of the man who lived there, of the times he saw, and the thoughts and prayers with which he must have struggled.

Just as the island is pleasingly close but steadfastly unreachable, so are the facts behind the oratory's stones, its doors and windows, its carefully constructed sheep fold, enough information to intrigue, too little to satisfy the curiosity.

As if to contrast with the serenity of the island, Bird Rock is all action with birds flying in all directions off its long sloping side, like a triangular sail on an old sailing ship, so close and so many, you would wonder how they avoid collision.

From the Dunlicky Rd, the noise is startling, an elemental crying to the wind and the sea, but from the Diamond Rocks, it's the movement which catches the eye, flickering, swooping and rising white spots, like foam from the rollers beneath, with no rhyme or reason to their direction, performing in a silent movie of activity, out of earshot, and lost in the sound of the waves.

So many birds on Bird Rock, so few around the island. Another Kilkee mystery – at least to me.

From my first visit to Kilkee, the Diamond Rocks have been a special place, and, like so much else in the town, at first, my friends and I thought, it was our unique discovery! It is a place which brings peace while forcing you to contemplate the vastness of time, the power of the sea, and the remorselessness of geology, as rocks slip, and rise, and weather, and fall, and change their shape and consistency, and keep within them the story of their ageing. I know of nowhere that tells this tale more beautifully or with as much clarity. At the Diamond Rocks you are sitting in a cradle of history, and it never fails to be awe inspiring, no matter the weather, the season, or the state of the tide.

In another ironic nod to those readers under forty, it makes me smile now to remember how we would take a battery powered record player to this place, find a sheltered and flat rock and play 45 rpm vinyl singles as an accompaniment to our picnic or conversations. It is the technology of a different age, and, compared to the ease of transporting downloaded music on an iPod today, it seems a ridiculous exercise.

In 1969, one of our favourite holiday tunes was Jimmy Webb's "Galveston", sung by Glen Campbell. With its lyrics about "sea waves crashing" and "sea birds flying", it really fitted at the Diamond Rocks. I remember lying back and listening to it one hot August day and thinking that you could make a great film around these cliffs – before I knew anything about the filming that MGM had carried out on just this spot over the previous winter. The ignorance of the visitor often becomes clear to me when I think back to my early days in the town.

Nowadays, I would never dream of importing music into this concert hall of nature, despite enjoying my mp3 player. The wash of the sea, the cry of the birds, and the buffeting of the winds make an important connection to the enormity of what is around me – I would never seek to drown out the natural sounds of this special place. But maybe that's the difference between youth and age.

If I close my eyes now I can picture dozens of ledges and shelves at the Diamond Rocks, where they are situated, the views they give, how comfortable they are for sitting on, and how to find them. The place is rooted in my mind and heart, like Kilkee itself.

When we had decided to go up Lookout Hill, we would seldom detour to the Diamond Rocks. We knew from experience that time could be lost there, and once you had been taken in by its waves and shapes and movement, plans for later might have to be abandoned when you finally checked your watch.

I have said that, in my memory, people did not go in as much for "walking" back in the sixties. Certainly it never felt busy on the cliffs to the west of the town, though you would often pass couples or individuals. However, the well trodden path up Lookout Hill testified to the fact that many followed that route, and, indeed, Mary John Knott refers to it in her mid 19th century book, and, of course, for decades it was, as its name suggests, the lookout point for the local coastguards; it was from the top of Lookout Hill that the distress of the Intrinsic was first spotted.

The path in the 1960s was well defined but not particularly formal. What fencing there was could be basic and intermittent, and the red brown clay was often slippery in wet weather or crumbling in dry. It was not a walk you would attempt with very young children, and maybe that explained the lack of passers by. I suspect the local folk now use the walk regularly, especially, perhaps, outwith the Summer season, and reports suggest that the paths on the cliffs are far more regularised and safety proofed than was the case all those years ago. Either way, it was a steep old climb to the top.

Once there, the effort was rewarded. As you would expect from "Lookout Hill", the view was magnificent. Looking back down over the fields to the West End, you could see the Duggerna Reef, part of the Bay, and the roofs of the town – and opposite the high rise of George's Head, Byrnes's Cove, and the wash around the cliffs at Farrihy Bay and in the distance, the Aran Islands – like ghostly mountains from another time.

Ahead of you was the view down the peninsula towards Loop Head, fields, cliffs, coves and rocks. An elemental depiction of the west of Ireland; a landscape which interrogated you and those things you believed important. How does all your busy life match up to the rugged endurance and ancient memory of this Nature, these rocks and waves, and ghost villages inhabited by overgrown memories?

I was always reminded of Lookout Hill when I heard Christy Moore sing "The Cliffs of Dooneen" and its line about the "high rocky mountains on the west coast of Clare" – hyperbole, perhaps, but redolent of this magnificent place.

To stand on the height of this cliff is life affirming and exhilarating; the wind which blows in your face also blows through your mind. If I was a GP in Kilkee, I am sure I would be tempted to prescribe the cliff walk as an initial answer to all minor complaints, so invigorating are its views.

Eventually, of course, you were faced with the need to turn back, and the choice between retracing your steps along the cliffs, with the encouragement of a possible can of lemonade or a chocolate bar at the Pitch and Putt shop, or a continuation of the walk down across the fields ahead and on to the Dunlicky Road.

Often the latter was our decision: partly because it got you back to the West End more quickly, but also because it was an interesting route.

Nowadays, I am sure there will be a clearly marked footpath from the foot of Lookout Hill to the road, but my memory of the sixties is that you had to meander across the field until you found your way on to the road.

What made this route interesting was that you passed along a road of houses where local people lived, rather than the holiday lodges down around the strandline.

There were the symbols of every day life strewn around, recognisable from your own life at home: children's toys, washing lines, ornaments in windows, perhaps a glimpse through an open door of a hallway with coats hanging, shoes lined up, or a dog barking at a gate, a parent calling a child. It was, in some way, enhancing of your holiday to be around people for whom Kilkee was home, and everyday, and "normal".

Occasionally you would pass someone getting in or out of a car, or hanging out washing, or cleaning their windows, and the face would be familiar – a waitress in the hotel, a barman, the guy who worked in the Central Stores – and seeing them away from their job somehow added another layer to your knowledge of the town.

The other thing that the Dunlicky Road added to our understanding of Kilkee, albeit as outsiders, was something which is common to many parts of the west of Ireland – something I think of as "generational architecture".

Though there has been much building along this road in recent times – as there has all over Kilkee – even in the sixties, you would often see a familiar sight: the original family cabin now used as a barn or cattle shed, the thatch long replaced with corrugated iron; next to it the utilitarian "modern" house, often two storeyed, built in the thirties or forties, and finally, the "new" house – closer to a bungalow, with a bit of garden landscaping around it. It was a fascinating and graphic demonstration of development through the generations, and I often wondered how often the people who lived there would think about the history of these houses, the family events which took place, and the rootedness of living so close to the homeplace of great and great great grandparents. Maybe, as part of their everyday life, the fascination of the position was invisible – but in a world which, even then, was starting to become much more mobile, with fewer people cleaving to their homeplace, it was something which I always found thought provoking.

Arriving back at the West End, depending on the time of day, we might go into the West End Stores for an HB ice cream, or perhaps into the Hydro bar for a shandy, followed by a bit of sunbathing in the hotel garden – the simple stuff that makes for happy and relaxing holidays.

As I write this now, it occurs to me that, especially before we had a car, there were parts of Kilkee, small as it is, into which we never ventured.

Albert Place, for instance, right next door to the Hydro Ballroom is a street that, to this day, I have never walked – though we would often see Fr Culligan when the priest's house was there.

Apart from our nocturnal visits to the O'Malley lodge, to play music in the dark, we never ventured down Geraldine Place, and though we happily stopped on Marine Parade to go upstairs at Murphy's café and bakery to sample some wonderful cakes, I don't ever remember going down Well Rd at the side of the Victoria Hotel. Of course, readers should remember that much of the building at the end of these roads, such as Well Field did not exist in those days, and, as such, there was little reason to head down the dead end streets.

Again, before we had access to a car, there was little reason for going down Church Rd, which was a lot less built up than it seems to be today. I do remember one occasion when a group of us, in town out of season, decided to go looking for our pal, Cyril Costello, who was a waiter at the Hydro Hotel. He lived on Church Rd and when we knocked on the door his mother was somewhat mystified to see us standing there; Cyril was equally bemused when he came to the door to find a group ready to greet him!

On the other hand, we had many reasons for going along Circular Rd, not least the Post Office and John Williams Pharmacy. The Marine, of course was there, and Peg O'Halloran's shop, and we sometimes took a short cut along Post Office Lane.

The major reason for going up Circular Rd would be to go to church. When we were in Kilkee for most of August, that might mean four Sunday Masses plus a Holiday of Obligation for the Assumption on August 15th. Many who see the church these days must be amazed at its size and capacity, but, back in the sixties, there was no problem filling it up three or four times every Sunday. For me, it was very different to the experience of going to Mass at home: the size of the place, the echoing public address system, the rumble of the responses from over a thousand in the congregation. It felt like being in a place of pilgrimage – like Lourdes, perhaps.

The church building was only three or four years old when I first went to Kilkee, an incongruously modern barn of Faith. Fr Kenny was a remote figure with a microphone, but I remember he had a particular talent in his sermons for combining the spiritual and the temporal, and he would always end by wishing for "glorious weather" to encourage the visitors.

Realistically, I suppose it was not an atmosphere in which piety was encouraged – too big, too much echo, too many people. It also has to be admitted that it was often at Mass where you would catch a glimpse of a face you would be hoping to see in the Hydro Ballroom later that day, and also, a good look at her family! It was probably sacrilegious, but I would be pretty sure I wasn't the only teenager in the church who was in receipt of a hurried smile, a blush, or a secret wink as the long lines went up and down to Communion.

It was my first glimpse of the way the Irish did Mass and I found it quite fascinating. Rightly or wrongly, I always found great comfort to be part of a large crowd all heading to church before Mass; it was a kind of uniformity I was unused to at home, where the majority would not be Catholic, and, as for any community occasion, the sense of humanity heading in the same direction for the same reason, streets filled with bodies with a shared destination, was both positive and uplifting for me, like you might find on an All Ireland match day.

I was fascinated by the sight of the local men, gathered in the car park rather than in the church, and discussing cattle prices and racing bets rather than listening to the sermon. It seemed odd that they would make the effort to come to church and then not bother to step inside. Years later I heard Leitrim's John McGahern musing about religion in the west of Ireland. His view was that Catholicism was a kind of social control and that you needed to be seen fulfilling your duties, but that when folk went home, their actual core beliefs, superstitions and traditions, had not really changed that much from pre-Christian times: an interesting premise!

Be that as it may, and acknowledging the great changes which have come over the Church's position in Irish life over the past half century, I enjoyed going to church in Kilkee, and, I have to say that, years later, standing in the doorway of a crowded church in Baile an Fheirtéaraigh in the Corca Dhuibhne Gaeltacht, trying my best with the responses in Irish, while high above birds sang in summer sunshine, was probably my most spiritual experience ever!

There is a lot of building around the church and off Circular Rd now, but, in the sixties, there was only the Convent, which also contained the local girls' secondary school. It made for a peaceful area, and a good spot from which to see the old station and think of the West Clare Railway.

After Mass, or on other occasions when we had gone up Circular Rd, I used to enjoy the walk along Chapel St. It was a wide road with individually decorated low lodges and, in those days, little traffic. The design echoed much of the newer parts of the town around the Square when the local landowner rebuilt it on "estate town" lines, with wide streets and neat, if small, cottages.

O'Connell St was not a place I spent a lot of time, unless waiting for the bus, which would stop outside what was the Oifig an Fáilte in those times. The market in the Square did not attract me but I do remember some great set dancing there to the famous Kilfenora Ceilidh Band during the family festival one year.

We were quite familiar with Grattan St and often took a walk down Erin St to look at the old fire engine in the Fire Station and cut down the alley at the side to the Strandline.

It strikes me at this distance that we were more at home in the West End and on O'Curry St than we were in the East End of the town. This was probably because we stayed towards the West End mostly, but I still feel that attraction to the West more than to the East.

However, that is not to say that we ignored the East End.

We would enjoy the walk around past the Strand and the Thomond, the usually abandoned air of the Dutch with its faded pastel balconies, and curtains blowing through broken windows, the bungalow owned by Dessie O'Malley, and the ancient, half derelict, Atlantic Lodge.

The pier area was a little less finessed than these days and there was often some interesting work going on with fishermen or divers, or maybe an upturned namhóg, currach, or canoe, as they call them here.

Sitting on the slipway, with your back to the harsh, rough concrete of the pier, and the orange lights, reflected in the sea, circling the bay ahead of you, like the columns of some Greek temple, was a great way to end the day after a long session in the Hydro Ballroom. Few walks are as romantic as that followed by couples around Moore Bay at 2am!

We were never sure if we were welcome in the Golf Club. In those days it had quite a small lounge area, and, even when word got round that there was to be a "session" there, there was always a hesitance about going up and knocking on the door. I think the feeling was that it was really for those who golfed there, and they didn't want to attract the attention of the guards by having too many, too obvious, lock ins! Nevertheless, there were a few occasions when my mother would greet me at breakfast by saying that I'd missed "a great session in the Golf Club last night."

The pitch and putt course there was situated on the town side of the clubhouse and was really quite steep. I played there a couple of times but never enjoyed it quite as much as Haugh's in the West End.

There were a couple of coves to explore in the cliffs near here, and that shelter I remember sleeping in for a couple of hours one early morning when it really was too late to return to the hotel. There was also a grassed area where cars could park but it was rare to see more than two or three. Likewise, the area at the bottom of the road, in front of Allender's Field, which is now dedicated to car parking, was far smaller then, and seldom overflowing, outside of peak holiday weekends. There were fewer cars around, and the idea of parking restrictions and traffic wardens would have been laughable.

The original GAA field as I knew it, was up the hill behind the Dutch. I remember going up there one year when there were community sports for the Family Festival, and a couple of the Keating girls came in from Kilbaha to take part in the traces; it was good to be part of a community event like that. That's a part of Kilkee life that many of the visitors miss out on I would think.

At the end of the road was a small flat grassed area where cars would occasionally park, and then there was the walk over the small bridge on to George's Head itself.

The choice then became the low road or the high road.

To go high meant basically climbing the steep slope of the Head till you reached the edge of the cliffs far above. There you could lie flat on a low ledge below the meadow's edge and contemplate the breakers far below, or you could gaze across to the Diamond Rocks and the West End – the whole town seemingly laid out like a model on a map.

From there you could head even further up the hill, head on towards Farrihy and Corbally and come to the village of Coosheen. In the late sixties, the former National School was opened as a folk museum and a "fisherman's cottage" constructed. It was in a stunning location and I remember visiting shortly after it was opened and being impressed by the care that had gone in to its establishment. I have seen no mention of the museum for many years and so suspect it may have closed, but it is encouraging to see Coosheen and Corbally referred to as 'heritage areas" in literature associated with the "Wild Atlantic Way". If life can be preserved in such places, there is hope for all!

Had you taken the low road at the bridge on to George's Head you would eventually have reached the top of the cliffs – but first you would have had to pass above "Burns's Cove" or "Byrnes's Cove" as it now seems to be.

In simple terms, this was a fairly sheltered cove, with big enough waves to make swimming interesting, partially obscured from the land around it. This was presumably a reason why it was designated an area which allowed naked male bathing. If I recall correctly, it had a small shelter where men could change out of their clothes and a small rocky beach. If I'm honest, that's a description which may be awry – because I was never brave enough to have a good look at the place.

We were, allegedly, teenagers of the, ahem, "happening generation". Musicals like "Hair", featuring full frontal nudity were on the West End stage, our parents were terrified of what we might be getting up to with our long hair and wild music.........except.......

156

For virtually everybody I knew, it was not like that at all. We may have had "different music" and be dressed less conservatively than our parents' generation, but for most of us, school, study and a relatively "normal" lifestyle was the everyday reality. And I guess our reaction to Burns's Cove was as good an illustration of that, and of the spirit of the times, as anything.

Just passing above the cove would reduce us to hysteria. Would we see a naked man? Would he see us? What would he look like? Would he be angry or embarrassed? There would be hurried looks and muffled shrieks – though we seldom saw anyone bathing there. I think early morning and early evening were probably the chosen times for the regulars – probably in the hopes of avoiding screaming and giggling teenagers. The innocence of their naked bathing and our reactions seems to belong to far more than half a century ago. The rumour was that the Christian Brothers who holidayed in the town were particular devotees of this facility. Again, with the knowledge of later years, something may have been made of this, but then, it was simply an added frisson to the repressed reactions we employed whenever we were nearby.

I was taught by the Christian Brothers, and, for most of the time, was sensibly terrified of them. I had neither the desire to see them naked nor the ability to even imagine the possibility – now that really would have needed mind altering drugs!!!

They were such different times.

The other attraction of George's Head was the presence of cattle and the endless chats about why they would be on what part of the grassy slopes, and if it had any relevance to the coming weather. You also had to watch where you were walking – which could be quite an experience for city kids!

It was often when we were returning from George's Head that we would take a short cut across the strand. Though I had friends who had promised their parents they would take a swim in the sea every day they were in Kilkee, I don't remember spending a lot of time actually on the strand – other than to play long games of football or cutting back across to the West End, always needing to find a way to cross the stream that ran over the sands from under the bridge near the Victoria Hotel. Beach sports and pastimes like surfboarding were not common in the sixties and you would really go on to the strand only if you were going to swim or if you wanted to sunbathe and make sandcastles. I preferred the comfort of a deckchair in the Hydro garden or a place on the rocks in front of the West End Hotel by the bathing shelter, or somewhere else in the West End, for taking the sun.

I loved looking at the strand though – its smooth shell shaped, semi circle could be quite hypnotic, especially as the light changed on it as the day passed, and I sometimes took a solo walk there in the early evening, especially in later years when I was in the town. In those teenaged years, I was maybe too busy to appreciate its calm and soothing elements. However, even for a busy teenager, sunset always had the power to stop you in your tracks, and the lights reflected as orange pillars in the tide after dark were compelling and atmospheric. Nowadays a walk on the strand would be a daily routine if I was in Kilkee.

If I had been on the strand, I would often climb up off the sand using the slipway opposite the West End Stores – it was years before I discovered that the Stores had been Kilkee's first lifeboat station, and the slip the original means of launching the boat. You would have to say that the slip was well built and remained substantial right the way through the century.

That route would take me up to my favourite spot on the wall – just across the road from the Hydro gardens, along from the racquets courts and ideally placed to watch the bay, or the people moving between town and the West End or vice versa.

But there will be another chapter on that particular joy!

160

OUT THE ROAD

As, strictly speaking, this is a memoir concerning Kilkee around the time of the 1960s, any accounts of places around Kilkee or Clare with which I became familiar are not fully relevant, though they do provide a context for my holiday memories.

In the early years, as I have said, without a car, we tended to stay most of the time in Kilkee itself, except for the outings on which we were taken by P.J. King in his trusty taxi.

Some of these were day long excursions. As mentioned, P.J. took us for our first visit to Corca Dhuibne, where we fell in love with Dingle and the road to Slea Head and the Blaskets, and discovered yet more Ryan's Daughter locations. On that trip, Killarney, Inch Strand and Lady's View also featured, and at various times we visited the Burren, Ard-na-Crusha, Killaloe and Bunratty.

P.J.'s local connections got us into the Loop Head lighthouse, before it was officially open to the public – and through trips out west, we got to know Moveen, Kilbaha, Ross and Moneen, Carrigaholt, Cross, Kilballyowen, Fierd, Doonaha and Querrin.

The Ryan's Daughter connection came in to play again – though we had visited the Bridges of Ross before we had seen their starring role in the Storm on the big screen. Our friend, Cyril Costello, was able to tell us that the dramatic and rocky cove where Leo McKern, as Tom Ryan, lost his glass eye, and saw his stand-in break a leg as huge breakers overwhelmed them, was situated at Goleen, a deep inlet close to the road, out towards Cross. When we first visited, some of the wooden rafts, on which the gunrunners' cargo of weapons in the film had been floated, were still lying about. The scene in the film where the huge wave crashes over the rocks, drowning both actors and camera, retains its power even today, and standing on the spot where it was filmed is to be reminded of the power of the sea – an fharraige mhór áibhéalta!

This early exposure to the Loop Head peninsula proved an attractive taster for what would be many later visits and wanderings around the area through the years, and I grew to appreciate the lanes and fields of this part of west Clare and the particular atmosphere they created.

I love walking out the Dunlicky Road till I am opposite Bird Rock and Bishop's Island, lying on the springy turf and losing myself in the acrobatic displays of the wheeling seabirds. Every season and all types of weather have their own attractions – even in rain and storm, the grandeur of breakers and foam on the rocks, before you and below you, makes it worth suffering a soaking. Looking out to Bishop's Island, it is hard to avoid second guessing the contemplations of Senan as you view the remains of his oratory and his sheep fold

In warm summer sun, though that ocean breeze is always present, the dazzle of a shining sea, the blue of the skies reflected in the waters below, and the vivid colours of flowers, earth, and turf in the sloping fields is life affirming. The pattern of walls and fences, and the long narrow grey lanes, often mixed with the greens of moss and grassy banks or ditches, is quite bewitching and holds the eye to the impossibly far horizon.

The road rises as you drive into Cross and you are welcomed by the busyness of houses, the GAA field, shop, pub and the national school. There are new and renovated houses alongside the road, the pinks and yellows bright against the green of the fields and the blue, white, or greys of the sky.

When I first came to west Clare, this part of the peninsula told a story of history; it was a poster for emigration, for families long gone, and dreams shattered. A gate half covered by hedge growth would conceal a short path, unwalked for years, to a weathered front door, glassless windows, and a roof open to the elements, no longer covering a hearth that was no longer the heart of a home.

People may close doors and walk away from family homes, but their history, their births and deaths, their marriages and celebrations, their farewells and greetings, the enveloping atmospheres of lives lived through joy and grief, hope and despair, seldom leave.

Overwhelming it was, to stop in the silence of a lane, to try and work out the years the people had gone by the condition of their house, to see the signs of family history – the holly tree for Christmas decorations, the smoothness of the often turned handle on the still shut front door, net curtains gone cream with age behind half blind windows – their sight obscured by the dust and wind of decades.

It always felt like being in the presence of something, or someone; you would hesitate to speak or even make a noise; you would almost freeze – straining to hear the echoes, wanting the people to be there after all, trying to deny history with the willpower you would use to pull open a rusted gate.

In those early days, the graveyard at Kilballyowen, though still in use, presented an overgrown feel as the weathered gravestones clustered round the ruins of the roofless church. Often, only the surnames could be deciphered, telling their tale of the locality with the Keanes, the Keatings, the Carmody and McMahon families, Geaneys and Considines, all forever in Kilballyowen, reminders of a strong people in a windswept landscape.

The clusters of family names assert the connection with the land, and it would be a brave, ignorant, or foolish person who would attempt to portray the folk of this peninsula as romantic heritage figures. Heaving kelp up from the beaches to fertilise the fields, digging hard to keep boggy fields drained, clinging to community to balance the remoteness of the location – none of these options are for the faint hearted, I would say.

In the mid nineteenth century, this land supported over eight thousand souls, till famine, cholera, and the boat to America decimated the population. Nowadays there would be around two and a half thousand folk on the peninsula to add to the eleven hundred or so in Kilkee.

My more recent visits suggest a new vitality in the area. Like my own area in Leitrim, it seems that many remote areas are these days peopled by many people who have chosen to be there, and have a commitment to the land and its revival. Sustainable tourism, food and drink, crafts and arts, as well as farming and service industries are resurgent in this part of west Clare and must be hopefully saving the area from further decline.

Good work is being done by locals and incomers, awards are being won for promotion of the area which is clearly being carried on in an ethical and considered manner, and with the support and involvement of those who live there. The balance between holiday homes and homes for local folk, the fight for decent infrastructure and support, and the need to modernise without losing the area's past and traditions – these are all battles familiar to people in remote parts in many countries. The Loop remains remote despite the internet and improved transport possibilities. The trick is, I suppose, to maintain the attraction of its remote situation whilst building opportunities which will help young people to stay and make a living in the area should they choose to do so.

It is further west and more remote than Kilkee itself – but must face the same problems, and find its own solutions. It would be nice to think that the success of the Wild Atlantic Way will contribute to Ceann Léime moving into the 21st century without losing the atmosphere which makes it so special.

Heading "behind", as they would say in Kilkee, has many happy memories for me. One of my options, were I to be forced to portray Paradise, would be based on a warm September evening in the early seventies, sitting with a pint on the wall across the road from what was then "Haiers" and is now "The Lighthouse" in Kilbaha, watching the sunset over the bay.

The story of the "Little Ark", now housed at the church in Moneen, never fails to remind me of the struggles of our forefathers. For those unaware of the story: in the mid nineteenth century when the saying of Mass was prohibited in the area by the landlord, the local priest, Fr Meehan, seeing a "bathing machine" on the strand at Kilkee, had an idea for providing Mass for the people. He had an "ark" constructed – basically a small hut on wheels into which an altar was placed. This was towed out at Kilbaha strand so that it was situated between the low and high tide marks, where the landlord's writ did not run, and the people could gather round and join with the priest in celebrating Mass and the sacraments.

165

Looking at the structure today, preserved in Stella Maris church in Moveen, is to ponder on the Faith of the people and the ingenuity of the priest.

My own personal interest in the Star of the Sea church is that, apart from Fr Meehan's grave, there is also the grave of Fr Barney Keating – the priest who served the people of Liverpool for years, and, in so doing, "gave me" Kilkee – which does make it a place of pilgrimage for me!

Carrigaholt was a sleepy village when I first knew it, largely notable for the local Irish College, Coláiste Eoghain Uí Chomhraídhe, and in our case, for the cosy atmosphere of Pearse Fennell's pub, which in those days felt more like somebody's front room. For a long time, at the cross in Carrigaholt, there was a large barrel, with a pair of legs sticking up out of it, as far as I can recollect, without any explanation.

Returning to Kilkee gave you a choice of roads: the low road would take you virtually along the beach towards Doonaha, while the higher road turned up towards Moyarta and up past the cemetery.

This peaceful area was also a reminder that when you have a long association with an area, as happy as your memories will be, you form an attachment which means you also share the sad times. One of the staff at the Hydro had been Martina Scanlon from around here – really one of the nicest folk you could meet – and her family had suffered tragedy when her brother had been killed young in what I believe was a tractor accident; even Fennell's Bar had been the scene of a fatal accident not long after I started visiting, when, according to my recollection, a gas bottle had exploded. People lost whom I did not know or I had never met still remain in my thoughts because of my love of where they lived.

It is in the nature of country areas anywhere, but particularly by the sea, that people are lost before their time in farming or marine incidents, and it is a sad fact of rural Irish life, and its reporting, that nowadays I am most likely to notice a mention of places so close to my heart when a serious traffic accident is detailed, or an accident at sea, often involving young people.

I always try to remain aware, and have tried to do so in compiling this memoir, that the places I loved were not merely there as a backdrop to happy times in my life, but existed as the homes of families and residents whose lives were fully lived there and not just for weeks of the year. For all that, when sadness comes to places as beautiful as these, the contrast between sorrow and beauty becomes very poignant.

Towards the end of the sixties, when some of our friends had access to cars, we enjoyed more trips out west and to the Bridges of Ross.

Some moments resonate down through the years.

One September I stayed with a pal in a house his parents owned at Spanish Point. In the morning we walked down to the pier, bought some fresh landed mackerel, and cooked them in butter. Has to be the finest breakfast I've ever had!

I visited the Willie Clancy week a couple of times and remember sitting in Hillery's pub absolutely captivated by a family – parents and children - from Mayo – who just played and sang the whole night. They were marvellous – and every time the door opened, music would flow in from folk who were playing on the pavements and sitting on the roadside along the main street of Milltown Malbay. I was pleased when my son's first ever drink in a pub (a glass of Guinness) was in Hillery's: a nice moment of continuity! Another year there was a drive up to Lisdoonvarna to see Christy Moore perform in Lisdoon's Hydro Hotel – a predictably wonderful night.

From when I was fourteen till my thirties it was as if West Clare had a selection of gifts to give me, which it handed out each time I visited, wrapping them in memories to be with me for the rest of my life.

No wonder Kilkee is special to me!

WHEN YOU ARE LEAST EXPECTING IT.......

Recently, an old school friend of mine asked what I was currently writing. I explained that it was a memoir of my holidays as a child in Kilkee. His reply surprised me:

"Oh aye – you were always talking about that in school. I used to wonder what it was like and where it was."

In those two sentences, I suppose, we have displayed the difference between the world before the internet and the world after.

In those days, to research a subject – or to find out about a place – you would need a visit to the library or bookshop, a search through the index, and a hunt for related pictures. Compared to the instant click on a search engine, it was a fairly time consuming and laborious activity.

My friend had no way of knowing about Kilkee, and, indeed, other than my mother, and Fr Keating, who we saw irregularly, I had nobody to whom I could talk about the town and have them recognise my references. The small group of friends who met up at the Hydro each summer would keep in touch by letter – and it was always a treat to arrive home from school and see familiar handwriting on an envelope on the mantelpiece, and know there would be another round of reminiscences from Surrey, London, Belfast or Coleraine.

As to news of Kilkee – it was virtually impossible to come by, from year to year. In an age when a picture of a storm wrecked sea wall on the Strandline is instantly available, or when a camera at the Diamond Rocks Café can let us watch live as breakers hit the reef, this seems hard to believe – but it was true. In fact, one of the excitements as we arrived in the town each August was to look around and see what had changed and what had stayed the same – we would have had no way of knowing whilst we were at home.

That is not to say, of course, that Kilkee was out of mind. Scarcely a day would pass without a reminder of our holiday – a song on the radio, a faint scent of seaweed on a beach, a soft ice cream like the ones they sold at the Arcadia, an Irish accent on television, scorecards or bright yellow tees from the Pitch and Putt found in a pocket – they all tugged at the memory, and the heartstrings. On my iPod today, you will still find a playlist entitled "Hydro Ballroom Songs" – everyone of them spinning me back to the mid sixties, to the sound of a rocking brass section, and the expertly turning couples at the foxtrot or jive, to the heat of the hall, the dappled reflections of the mirrorball, and the excitement of the moment.

Kilkee, though, had a habit of making sure you didn't forget her – as if you could!

I have said throughout this memoir that, in the early days, I was firmly convinced that I alone had discovered Kilkee, and that nobody else loved the town like I did. Oh the blind arrogance of youth! If the internet has done nothing else, it has confirmed that the town is much loved by thousands all around the world.

However, because of my misconception, it was always a shock when references to Kilkee suddenly entered the "real world" of everyday life.

When I returned to Edinburgh in 1970, to my birthplace and to university, I was probably at the height of my initial infatuation with Kilkee. I had been there, as usual in August, and returned for ten days in September, prior to starting student life. There was no way I would introduce myself to new friends without Kilkee featuring strongly in my introductions.

In one gathering, late night and fuelled by a few beers, I was extolling Kilkee's virtues. Normally, my enthusiasm was such, that, eventually, even the most patient of pals began to glaze over, as my details and descriptions seemed to continue for ever. However, I noticed one new friend, a member of my tutorial group, a Liverpudlian who had gone to a Christian Brothers' school not far from mine, was nodding enthusiastically, and seemed to be agreeing with many of the points I was making. His name was Frank Downes, his extended family were well settled in Bealaha and West Clare, and I recall him saying, his uncle and aunt had a connection with Taylor's pub in Moyasta.

Frank knew the area well, he had spent childhood holidays there and shared my enthusiasm for this part of the country. It was an early indication that my affection for, and knowledge of, Kilkee was not as unique as I had originally thought.

Generally, as with Frank, the Kilkee "link" came without warning. I remember settling down to watch an early Aisling Walsh film called "Joyriders", about a troubled woman and her slightly dangerous new boyfriend, seeking an escape from their Dublin blues.

171

Out of nowhere, in answer to his question of "Where will we go?" once he has "acquired" a car, she says:

"Take me to Kilkee – I had my honeymoon in Old Moore's Hotel!"

And, right enough, after a few adventures along the way, the couple's car draws up and parks near the Bandstand in Kilkee – where there are further adventures with the manager of a local Ballroom, played by John Kavanagh – a fine actor whose name on the cast list attracted me to the film. Brief though its appearance was, it was a welcome surprise to see the town on the screen like that – and without any prior warning.

More often, the town leapt at you out of a book where you had no reason to expect its presence.

Reading a biography of Charles J Haughey, from, as I remember it, Bruce Arnold, the throwaway phrase appeared that the 'Baron of Kinsealy' would often "walk upon the cliffs of George's Head in Kilkee" when he had a difficult problem to consider.

Being a keen student of Irish history and contemporary politics, there have been other opportunities for Kilkee to put in a sudden unexpected appearance during my reading. Going through the diaries of that famous "Revolutionary Woman", Kathleen Clarke, I was surprised to find out that her husband, Tom, the old Fenian, whose signature was the first on the 1916 Proclamation, had proposed to her on a walk up Lookout Hill. Realising she was a member of a strong Republican family, the Daly's of Limerick, it made sense that she would be well acquainted with the town as a holiday spot, and it is nice to think that Tom was inspired enough by the views from high above Kilkee to summon the nerve to pop the question.

Some references are less easy to confirm. Many conspiracists suggest that one of the Littlejohn Brothers, allegedly British spies during the Troubles in the 1970s, was arrested after hiding out on a Kilkee caravan site. More ascertainable is the bizarre story of Sean Bourke – who did live in a caravan, albeit near the old Railway Station in the town, and who had been a part of the escape plan of Russian spy/British double agent George Blake from Wormwood Scrubs Prison. A link between Kilkee and the Cold War was totally unexpected – to this observer, anyway.

However, a later discovery almost suggests a trend!

Apparently, there had been rumours of a famous visitor at the Strand Hotel, but little in the way of firm evidence until a certain guest book for 1961 was investigated, and the name "Rafael Trujillo" was identified as an alias used by Che Guevara to avoid the attentions of the CIA. Sure enough, he had stayed in Room 3 on September 12th 1961.

The story is that Che and a party were on an Aeroflot flight from Prague to Cuba which had touched down at Shannon and become fogged in overnight. The airline arranged for them to be accommodated at the Strand, and that is how the great revolutionary came to visit Kilkee – a good five years before I managed it!

The details of the story ring true to me as on more than one occasion a bus would arrive without warning at the Hydro – loaded with tourists whose plane had been delayed at Shannon for mechanical or meteorological reasons.

Guevara was apparently proud of his connections to the Lynches of Galway, and arranged to tour the Kilkee area while waiting for the weather to clear – in a Ford Prefect, of all cars!

This link between Kilkee and great world affairs intensifies when we hear about Che's late morning drink in the Marine Hotel Bar.

Unsure what to drink in Ireland, Che asked the rookie barman for advice and took a glass of Power's with some water, at his recommendation.

The barman was a lad called Jim Fitzpatrick, who later became a well respected artist, and six years later, a year after Che's death, he would produce the famous and iconic image of Che which has adorned a million tee shirts and bedroom walls, not to mention the racquets courts on the strand! And it all started in the bar of the Marine Hotel in Kilkee!

A couple of times, Kilkee has ambushed me when I've been on long haul flights to the States. I had bought a book called "Rathcormick" by Homan Potterton. It told of a middle class Protestant upbringing in 1950s rural Ireland and I had thought the view through a "different" prism of mid century Irish life might make for interesting reading. Bizarrely, when the flight would have been somewhere above the west of Ireland, I turned a page and realised he was about to give an account of his yearly summer holidays to stay in a lodge at the West End in Kilkee. His times in Kilkee had been around a decade before mine, but his feelings about the town and his vivid descriptions rang very true to me.

On another such flight, I was leafing through a British Airways flight magazine when I came across a piece on "favourite holiday spots" from various celebrities. Limerick's Terry Wogan was waxing lyrical about his childhood summers in Kilkee, not perhaps as surprising a link as that of Che Guevara, but nevertheless it was fascinating to read of familiar places and pursuits – details I had previously thought were special to me!

Given the size of the town, the number of links to the bigger world sometimes seemed remarkable.

When "Angela's Ashes" was published to great, if mixed, acclaim, one of the less gloomy areas of Frank McCourt's background turned out to be the annual trips to Kilkee when he was a boy scout. His brother, Malachy, a writer and teacher, commented on those summer visits as well, and there are photographs around showing the two of them on the strand, or sitting on the wall at the east end, as part of a clearly happy scout group.

When I picked up a recently published biography of Richard Harris by Limerick journalists, Michael Sheridan and Anthony Galvin, I was delighted to find that a major part of the text relied on Kilkee memories, particularly supplied by Manuel.

As you might expect, Manuel Di Lucia was often involved in these surprise appearances of Kilkee in the media. In the summer of 2015, on RTE, "John Creedon's Wild Atlantic Way" travelled the length of the West Coast – a coastline which, as Creedon reminded us, was described by Yeats as "the land of your heart's desire."

I wouldn't be disagreeing with that, and it was pure joy to sit in my living room and watch "Creedo" interviewing Manuel at the Pollock Holes, and receiving a good history lesson involving geology, the history of diving in the area, and the swimming initiation rites of thousands of children in Kilkee down through the years.

However, while these various references often came as a surprise to me, the truth was that Kilkee had attracted famous names almost since the start of its times as a bathing resort.

Tourism brochures had long pointed out that Ryder Haggard, writer of "She" and King Solomon's Mines" had carved his initials on the rocks near Edmond Point, and that the Crown Princess of Austria had visited the town. The poet, Alfred Lord Tennyson, famously stayed at Old Moore's Hotel, as did Thackeray, and, of course, Percy French, as mentioned, was a regular visitor.

In some ways, the strangest connection I discovered was when high on the Yorkshire Moors at Haworth parsonage. The home of the Bronte sisters is within a howling wind's distance of the reputed sites of 'Thrushcross Grange' and 'Wuthering Heights', it can be a melancholy place at the best of times as you look out from the sisters' bedrooms on to the graveyard and the dark, grey, houses stretching away down to the village beyond. In some ways, it is the opposite of Kilkee with its big skies and oceanic freshness.

However, here I read of Charlotte Bronte's stay in Kilkee on her honeymoon, with her new husband, the Reverend Arthur Bell Nicholl, from Killead, Co Antrim. Tom Byrne has written well on this subject, and the small mention of Charlotte's honeymoon to be viewed in the house at Haworth suggests that the wildness of the ocean raised Charlotte's spirits, and she certainly commented very positively on her stay in Kilkee in 1854 – where she spent the most time of any place on her honeymoon tour of the country. She was very complimentary of Mrs Shannon's West End Hotel – situated between Wellington Square and the Dunlicky Road, the establishment having moved there from Francis (Grattan) street as the town grew, and incorporating the Kilkee Post Office. The account in the parsonage finishes rather grimly: "She was to die within eight months of her honeymoon, having not yet reached 39 years of age, to the great grief of her new husband." There is more than a whiff of "See Kilkee and die!" about their report!

As was the custom in Victorian resorts, and still is today, I suppose, hotel keepers and advertisers were always keen to proclaim the names of the famous who had stayed at their establishments – though it is a timely reminder of the fleeting nature of celebrity that the names of many of the "imposing figures" listed from Kilkee over a hundred years ago would mean nothing to us today.

It is also interesting to note how the tourism business has a long history of "embroidering the facts" to attract visitors.

In our house, we had a copy of a 1950s "AA Touring Ireland" book. It was crammed full of maps and information about everything from market days across the country to the meanings of Irish place names. The entry on Kilkee was predictably full and fulsome in its praise. However, one paragraph has always remained in my memory.

The book stated that the polar explorer, Ernest Shackleton, had been born in Kilkee, and that "locals are happy to point out the typical low roofed, Kilkee seaside lodge where he had been born."

I was content for years to take this as fact, as a kind of equivalent for West Clare of West Kerry's own polar hero in Annascaul's Tom Crean. I thought to check out which of the "typical low roofed, Kilkee seaside lodges" Shackleton had actually been born in; the line drawing in the AA book suggested it may have been somewhere on Marine Parade – but I was never able to track it down.

This was not surprising, for, as I was later to learn, Shackleton had, in fact, been born at "Kilkea Castle" near Athy in Co Kildare – same sound, different spelling.

It was a lesson in how hearsay and tradition cannot always be trusted as accurate. I daresay some of my "received truths" about Kilkee and its people may be embroidered or wide of the mark. However, I think the point is that the town is the kind of a place which generates such affection that tales will be told, rumours repeated, and traditions formed which those of us who love the place hold dear to us.

Like family history, all of us have memories, stories and half captured moments from Kilkee; they comfort us in hard times and inspire us when we need strength. They remind us that, however bleak the view from where we are, there is a better place, with a better outlook.

For that reason, I know Kilkee will keep appearing in my life when I least expect it, like an old friend met in the street, or a faded picture dropping from the pages of a much loved book.

Who we were, and where we were, is part of who we are now.

"TO MANY PEOPLE, HOLIDAYS ARE NOT A VOYAGE OF DISCOVERY, BUT A RITUAL OF REASSURANCE"

Philip Andrew Adams

Writing at length about my Kilkee experiences and memories, I have inevitably been wondering about "holidays" – what they mean, why we enjoy them, how they affect us, and also how they have changed over the decades.

The concept of "holiday" or "re-creation", outside of the landed gentry, is a relatively recent idea. Before the industrial revolution, most folk worked on the land and their hours were regulated by the seasons, daylight, and the needs of the fields. Later, once the work force were in factories, from a young age they worked long hours and had only Sundays as 'the day of rest'. Timewise, economically, philosophically, and even in terms of logistics – the idea of 'ordinary folk' having 'holidays' was a non-starter.

The history of Kilkee as a holiday resort really is a reflection of the development of holidays and the vacationing behaviour of 'the masses'.

In the early days, one needed to be of a certain level of income to afford the arrangements to travel and to stay away from home. This might have involved a personal carriage, accommodation for servants, and, of course, a 'private income' which precluded the necessity for paid employment, thus making the time available for travel.

As already mentioned, it was first the provision of steamship passages from Limerick to Kilrush, and then the advent of the railway to Kilkee which really opened up the town to tourism. Logistically, it became possible for folk on an average income to reach Kilkee and return home on the same day – with no need for overnight lodgings: the era of the day tripper was arriving.

Eventually, car ownership revolutionised how people actually went on holiday, and probably heralded Kilkee's heyday as a thriving resort – especially given the availability of self catering accommodation, as well as hotels and guest houses.

After 1945, most folk had an expectation of an annual "holiday" – whether it was near to home or further afield, and, as we have seen, many Limerick folk established the tradition of summers in Kilkee.

From the late sixties onwards, with more accessible air travel, package holidays developed in Spain and Greece and other parts of Europe – and this, of course, had an impact on resorts like Kilkee.

At the turn of the millennium, budget airlines facilitated 'weekend breaks' and the idea of multiple holidays in a year become more accepted. Similarly, long haul holidays, not just to the USA but to Mexico and South America or Thailand and the Far East came within the reach of a larger part of the population.

At the same time, many people looked for "activity holidays", themed around a sport or pastime – and Kilkee has always been in a good position to offer diving and walking retreats.

With wider prosperity, and in Ireland this would equate with the period of the 'Celtic Tiger', the idea of a "second" or "holiday" home became more common, and whilst, with the lodges around the bay, there had long been such a tradition in Kilkee, as can be seen from the town today, the early years of this century led to a huge expansion in the building of houses for people to stay in while on holiday built to the standards by which they might live at home, rather than basic holiday accommodation.

The Crash, of course, brought a further change of direction as holidays and tourism were amongst the first casualties of reduced circumstances, and brought hard times to resorts at home and across Europe.

Holiday habits change rapidly these days, and resorts face the challenge between continual adaptation to reflect current trends, or a brave decision to remain unchanging and hope that enough of their customers will value the familiar to keep returning.

In a sense, this reflects the two alternatives offered by Andrews in his quotation at the start of this chapter – the reassurance of an unchanging place, or the excitement of new and different experiences. Whilst some adventurers would never dream of returning to the same location each year, because they crave "new" experiences, I suspect many holidaymakers seek a mixture of both the new and the familiar - but that is a difficult trick for the resort to pull off: to retain its familiar charm, whilst modernising to match the latest expectations. It is only too easy to end up having ruined the familiar and not being convincing enough with the new.

I am sure Kilkee has witnessed many, many hours of discussion along these lines: what do we change and what do we keep? What should be preserved intact, and which elements of a modern resort will fit in with our town and add to its attraction, without affecting the much loved charm of the original, Victorian, seaside place? As is the case in any retail situation, there is no way of being sure in advance which will be the more successful decision.

Likewise, holidaymakers have the choice to make: to return to the same well loved places, or to seek pastures new?

I suppose that the type of holiday we choose reflects our personality, the stage of our life, and the circumstances in which we find ourselves. After a frantic year, we may seek peace; if our life has been quiet, the excitement of distant places or challenging activities might be our goal.

This, I feel, tells us much about holidays and what they provide for us. The idea of recreation as in "re-creation" is central to a positive holiday experience. Doing familiar things against a different background, or new things in familiar surroundings, brings a freshness to our lives. Like a white portrait backed with a black mount – the contrast makes it stand out.

On holiday, we *can* re-create ourselves – the timid can become brave, the eternally busy can become reflective, the solitary may find friends, and the gregarious find an opportunity to be alone with themselves for a time. A change, they say, is as good as a rest, and the truth of that goes beyond a cliché. The physical and mental rest provided by the right holiday can prepare us for our return to the daily grind; the promise of a holiday ahead can give us the strength to keep going when we are low. One of the crucial aspects of a holiday is that it is personal to each of us; we all have ideal destinations and pastimes, we all choose our holidays, their location, timing, duration and content to suit ourselves – or our families and friends. As such, they are an extension of who we are, or who we would like to be. Our holiday choice reveals something about us, what is important to us, and, in a sense, how we might like to live our lives if they were freed from the constraints of work and routine.

In our youth, holiday time can represent the hopes and possibilities of our life ahead; in middle age, it can reflect our achievements and our current and family priorities, and later on in life, it clearly offers an opportunity to reflect and look back, as well as enjoy opportunities which may not have been available during our working life.

I met and became friendly with many people who were in Kilkee to work – either because it was their home place, or because they had come to the town for a summer job or for training in tourism or hospitality. I was always aware that they and I saw the town in a different way. For them, no matter how much they liked the place, it was, ultimately, the location for work and application to duty. When they joined with us in holiday activities, it was as a brief break from work, rather than as part of a two or three week break from "real life"

At times, I envied them – though I suspect I was always aware of the danger of replacing my "favourite holiday place" with a venue for work or home. Similarly, when people asked why I didn't go and live in Kilkee if I loved the place so much, I was quite clear about my answer.

My first reason was that the town was so dear to me that I always needed to have it as "somewhere to go to" when I needed a lift to my spirits or inspiration. If I lived there full time, it could not fulfil that important role in my life.

Secondly, I suspect that I did not want to be a "blow in". I was quite comfortable in my role as "that guy from Scotland, with a Liverpool accent, who loves Kilkee, and turns up at odd times." I did not want to become a resident in the town - who was neither native to Kilkee nor a visitor. I suppose I preferred being the foreigner who knew a surprising amount about the place, rather than the resident who was surprisingly ignorant about Kilkee.

If I am honest, the other reason why I never seriously contemplated moving to Kilkee was because I was afraid that our love affair would be tarnished by familiarity. For a few years in the early seventies, I guess I may have spent, annually, up to three months in the town at various times of the year. I was shy and quiet, and, as an only child, well used to, and comfortable with, my own company. I am sure there will be Kilkee folk reading this memoir who will have no idea who I am, nor how I come to be writing about them and their lives in such detail. I was content to observe and be on the peripheral; it was not in my nature to push myself into the centre of things.

As I have described previously, Kilkee and its people almost operated as a real life soap opera for me. I loved the setting - for its wild beauty and unpredictability, I loved the characters for their warmth and individuality – but I had no desire to jump on stage and pretend to be one of them. Much of my happiness in the town lay in the fact that Kilkee, and its people, appeared to be completely happy with that approach. They took me as they found me, and that suited me really well, because I just loved being there.

And, in reference to that headline quotation: each time I visited the town, I discovered more – about the place and, I suspect, about myself. I have no doubt that I was, to a certain extent, a different person in Kilkee to the child and man who studied or worked across the water – and that was obviously an attraction: that act of ongoing discovery – about myself, as well as west Clare – which meant I never felt I was merely repeating the holiday of the previous visit. The location might be the same, but the experiences would always subtly change – to meet my own needs and expectations.

At the same time, the familiarity of the place and its people, the comfort of knowing it was there and would be waiting for me, the individual history I had forged out of its memories and experiences, my happy personal geography in its streets, rocks, strand, and fields – all of those elements meant that my return to the town, whether in Spring, Summer or Autumn, formed a kind of "ritual of reassurance". It brought a chance to reconnect with a personal history that was important to me, to reflect on memories made when I was a child, to stand in the same places but view the world with different eyes, and, in so doing, to gain the perspective to try and work out if I was making the right choices and heading in the right direction.

As humans, we must develop and keep progressing, but we also possess the sentiment to regret what is left behind or lost when we move on. Often the things we do, or say, or desire, are linked to this conflict or contradiction: the need to change - in ways which benefit us, but to stay the same - in the ways which most make us happy and content. We would love to be able to reconcile the innocence of youth with the knowledge of adulthood: the optimism of initial efforts, with the grounded expectations provided by the passing years. We would love to retain the energy and innovation of the first half of our lives, whilst tempering it with the understanding and reflection of later years. As the French proverb states: "If youth only knew, and old age only could."

Surely, then, that is, in part what holidays are about? An opportunity to find the innocence in ourselves, or at least an opportunity to check if it still survives. The artificial shedding of responsibilities, the chance to escape from the demands of routine and expectations, the permission to be slightly careless and carefree: all of these represent at least a partial return to childhood, to that time when all things were still possible; when most decisions were reversible or less than crucial; when the weight of consequences was never so burdensome as to outweigh the vigour provided by impetuous, instinctive, or adventurous behaviour; when the urge to explore far outranked the admonition to be careful; when we felt alive in everything we did; when the moment was everything, and the future unconsidered, however briefly.

Kilkee, its places and people, provided the perfect setting for all of this re-creation: a safe haven for our dreams, a golden sun on a protected strand, a miraculous reef behind which the child could play safely.

It's not surprising we loved the place so well.

SITTING ON THE WALL

And so, in this memoir of Kilkee holidays, I have walked from Lookout Hill and the West End all around the bay, in and out of the lanes and streets of the town, and all the way up to George's Head.

I have retraced my steps, taking care to drop into a good few bars, guest houses, and hotels, - and now the sun is sinking towards the horizon, a child with his dog, and a runner with her evening thoughts, are casting long shadows on the strand, the occasional bird is flying noiselessly towards its last appointment of the day, and half familiar figures, alone or in couples, are strolling round the strandline, extras in my half century long love affair with Moore's Bay, its cliffs and hills, its houses and shops, and the people within them.

I walk past the metal gate near the top of the old slipway which used to launch the lifeboat down to the strand, I pass the West End Stores with thoughts of summer chocolate bars and melting ice creams, and I stretch slightly to look over the wall, at its highest point here, to see if anyone is taking advantage of a low tide, and the last of the light, to hone their racquets skills below. I can hear the swish of the racquets, the padding of the feet, and the slap of the ball – even when nobody is there.

I find the favourite spot, the very roughness of the stone on top of the wall is familiar and comforting, and, scuffing the heels of my shoes as I hoist myself up to sit there, I look up at the white building

187

at the top of the slope, its windows aflame with the setting sun's reflection, its outline as familiar to me as any building in my lifetime.

Do I see a young boy running across the grass in front of the hotel? Can I read his thoughts, his hopes, his fears? Is he familiar to me, and do I care for him and his future? Do I wish him happiness? Would I like him to notice me here: this man with his thoughtful face, and eyes half lost in memories, sitting on a wall which has protected his dreams for fifty years?

It is easy to capture the emotions such a vision stirs. They are as strong as the scent of drying seaweed which is brought like a rumour, from the sand and rocks below, by a gentle evening breeze, and seems to be looking for a curl of turf smoke with which to mingle.

It would be easy to mock the sentimentality of such a moment, to ridicule a lifelong love for a seaside town and a scattering of months filled with distant memories – but to do so would be to diminish life and love itself. Our interaction with what is around us is a part of what defines us as individuals. The memories we retain inform the decisions we make, and the way we react to others. The ability to look back as well as forward, rather than simply existing in the present, is one definition of our humanity.

For so many people around the world, memories of Kilkee (or indeed many, many, other holiday places) are the framework on which they hang their sense of childhood, the foundation for the adults they would become. When they think back to those days, they gain a stronger sense of themselves and the journey they have travelled.

Let me take you back to an August day in the late sixties, as you pass by this spot on the wall.

There is a group of us there: boys and girls, maybe five or six of us; the accents are diverse, the styles differ too. Perhaps we are involved in that most teenage of occupations – earnestly chatting – about everything or nothing; or maybe we are lost in thought, gazing out over the bay, or turning our heads to watch, as people pass by.

One thing you notice: we are beautiful!

Not in a glossy magazine, fashion shoot, ephemeral way – but the beauty that comes from the glow of being out in the sun, being relaxed and happy in each others' company, free from worries and responsibilities, living in the moment.

Of course, that's not to say we had no concerns: from exams looming, to whether that special person would notice us at the dance tonight – but, in general terms, our joy would possibly never be quite as innocent as this again.

With our lives before us, we could choose to take a wider or narrower view of our future. The same was true as we sat on the wall They said if you had a girlfriend, you would sit facing out into the bay – with the sweep of the strand and the big sky ahead of you, where the distant figures moving about became merely part of the landscape. However, if you were looking for a partner, the thing to do was to face inward, and hope to catch the eye of a passing girl.

There are places in the world which like to describe themselves as being "where the whole world passes by". You would never suggest that about the wall over the racquets alleys in Kilkee, but, in a sense, it was as if it did.

A semi circular bay, in a town at the end of the line, filled with holidaymakers, in times that were more relaxed and less frenetic than today, was a place of finite population. In those days, not many people "passed through" Kilkee. There were day trippers, it is true, but, generally, people came to Kilkee for at least a fortnight, and, in so doing, established routines – especially if they returned year after year. That was the "ritual of reassurance", referred to in the last chapter.

Listen to folk reminiscing about childhood holidays, and you can't fail to notice the repetition of "Remember how we always used to…". Part of the hotelier or retailer's skill would be to maintain that familiarity whilst subtly undertaking change at a rate which avoided the establishment being eventually seen as "old fashioned" or having failed to have "moved with the times". The tipping point could be very subtle, as many have discovered to their cost.

From the visitor's point of view, however, this "finite population" and these "rituals of reassurance" meant that a kind of microscosmic "world" was established in Kilkee for the duration of the holiday.

Many faces were familiar, even if the people were not known: the old couple who walked around the bay at 4pm, he with his walking stick, she with her sun hat; the young lad who emerged from the lodge on Marine Parade to run with the family dog on the beach at teatime; the two young girls half running, half laughing, as they headed for the Vic for their evening stint as waitresses; two elderly women, clearly sisters, who would walk arm in arm from Geraldine Place to the bandstand and back, each late afternoon, pausing every few yards to look out over the bay, occasionally pointing or exchanging a few words; the young family, dad teasing two young boys as they tried to keep control of a plastic football on the pavement, mum and daughter talking as they took turns with the pushchair containing the youngest family member; the clothes that were worn, individual choices but somehow linked by their holiday theme; the way that people walk when on holiday, positively without being focused, open to diversion, change of pace, or the odd skip or jump.

It was not hard to envisage the stories behind these people – the years they had visited the town, the progression from teenage to old age, the reasons for their daily routines, the anticipation of the annual Kilkee holiday, which we recognised so well. We may not have known these folk, these extras in our holiday world, but they were part of it, and would have been missed – in a vague and indeterminate way – had they not been there.

I have taken many people to Kilkee. Some have immediately understood its attraction for me, others have been mystified as to what made it so special in my life.

It is important to acknowledge that for many who go to Kilkee, it remains no more than a seaside resort – somewhere to picnic on the sand or on the rocks, to go for cliff walks, to play golf or dive, or to celebrate a stag or hen weekend. For these folk, the town plays no major part in their lives or memories; it is merely one spot in a list of possible holiday or weekend destinations. For the rest of us, however, and it is for those that I write this memoir, it remains something more than that, with more meaning in our personal histories.

For those who love Kilkee, the vital ingredient, of course, is that of human interaction: the time I spent there, the age I was when I first found the place, the role it played in my growing and developing, the associations with people and memories, discoveries and acknowledgements – those moments in life when we learn, or fail to do so, and upon which is built our future, our self awareness, and our motivation.

There is a sense in which I have always been sitting on that wall, or at least, have always returned to that familiar place – whether I happened to be physically in Kilkee or not. When I sat there first, I did so unconsciously, with not the slightest idea that I would be able to recall my times at that spot so clearly, so many years later. Because of that unconsciousness, those moments fulfilled an important role in my development – as a teenager and throughout my life.

It was there, I think, I first learned the art, the crucial skill, of being able to sit back and observe – the people and the scenes around you, but also yourself, your thoughts, your concerns. On the wall at the end of another perfect day, a calmness was accessible in the comfort of familiarity. It was where I sat, watching the people, the sun, the sky, the sea, and I rested there as naturally as anywhere. It became part of who I was, without my having any consciousness of its importance, or even its effect. We learn so much when we do so unconsciously.

There is something instructive about being still, while others pass by. Some evenings I would be there as part of a group: my holiday friends - united in our excitement; other times, I would find myself there alone, almost overwhelmed by a feeling of gladness that I *was* there.

Either way, it felt like all was right with the world, and I had the inspirational privilege of sensing that I was in exactly the right place at exactly the right time; filled with the certainty that I had no inclination or longing to be anyone but me, anywhere but here, any time but now. Maybe that's as good a revelation as any of what it means to be young.

And of course, there was the sea.

The rhythmic white noise of the coming and going of the tide was always there – sometimes almost hypnotically claiming your senses, at other times as a vague background murmur. It was reassuring – the fact that when it went out, it would always return, that the sound of the waves on the strand – either crashing or caressing – would not cease – wherever we were in the town, whatever time of day, however we were feeling.

The sea can help you realise your insignificance in the grand scheme of things, but it can also remind you of the privilege of being part of it all – and Kilkee certainly excels at that. Whether on the smooth sand of the strand, on the jagged teeth of the reef, or at the foot of the cliffs, boiling into caves and over rocks, the movement of the sea always echoes life in the town.

Its greatness gives us perspective; perspective gives us comfort.

I suppose what I am saying is that those three or four weeks in Kilkee each year gave us an opportunity to see the world, our world, more clearly – to see people rather than crowds, relationships rather than encounters, possibilities rather than inevitabilities. We were briefly taken out of ourselves, given an opportunity to look around, and when better for that to happen than in your formative, teenage years?

As we grow, increasingly we realise, it is those times "sitting on the wall" rather than "racing across the strand", which define us – who we are and how we face up to challenges and opportunities.

Kilkee gave so many of us the first period in our youth when we could reflect – on who we were, and what we wanted out of life. Because we felt safe, comfortable, energised, and relaxed, we could take the risk of thinking about the big issues.

The big dark August sky I was watching, as those shooting stars fell to earth, was a bigger sky in every way than the one I saw routinely in every day life. The performance of Justice Dunleavy and his songs of Percy French, was a new experience for me, the excitement generated by dances in the Hydro Ballroom was hitherto unknown to me, the people I met – from England as well as Ireland – widened my horizons, gave me a stronger sense of my own identity, and of my Irish connections.

Emotionally, the sun was brighter, the days longer, the sea a deeper blue. The grandeur of the cliffs, the power of the waves on the rocks, the ozone in the air, and the warmth of the breeze carried on the gulf stream – all of this acted upon me and I felt a surge of confidence in who I was and what I could do. Kilkee engendered a sense of well being in a way I had never found anywhere else. As I returned each year, I became more and more convinced that life was good, and a world which had such a place in it was a basis for optimism.

It was, therefore, an important part of growing, of adopting a positivity – a route to maturity, an opportunity to move towards being the person I felt I wanted to be. I am sure there are those who gained similarly from their holidays in other locations, - and indeed from a whole range of life events – but I can only speak for my own experience. As I have repeatedly suggested, in my own life and development, Kilkee was the right place at the right time. Without realising it, I was ready to take on board the messages it gave me. In short, I do believe that having spent so much time in Kilkee, I became, if not a better, then certainly a happier, person. We had a connection. I loved the way I felt when I was in Kilkee, and I have always been grateful to the town and its people because of that.

Of course, it is necessary to maintain a sense of perspective.

Looking back over fifty years, it is a reasonably easy task to identify the benefits I gained from my time spent in the town. Retrospective justification is not difficult, and I should concede that, in some respects, I am maybe over enthusiastic because of my happy memories.

The point is, of course, that they *are* happy memories. The weeks I spent in Kilkee *made* me happy, they brought joy, they gave me an exciting sense of discovery. They opened doors to a wider world and an older me. Without my Kilkee experiences, of course I would still have grown, still, hopefully, matured – but I'm not sure it would have been so much fun!

And that, perhaps, finally, is the main point to be made.

In my attempts to describe, explain, and understand why Kilkee has had such a hold on me, large parts of this memoir may have become analytical tracts. I may have given the impression that I wandered the streets and hills around the town with the furrowed brow of a furiously thoughtful philosopher. That would be nonsense! The very point of my happiness in Kilkee came from the sense of freedom it engendered, from the sheer fun I had, and my sublime ignorance of the importance these holidays would assume for me in the future.

The possibility that a holiday is something which enables you to find the child inside yourself – even as a teenager who is desperately trying to be grown up - was proved in my Kilkee experiences – and a lot of that was to do with the timing.

"The Sixties", as a concept, has become so manipulated by marketing gurus and faux historians that, for many of us who were actually there, current descriptions of the era are almost unrecognisable.

There may have been Hippies around Haight Ashbury in San Francisco, but for most of us who were teenagers in these islands, the sixties was about studying at school and playing records in our bedrooms.

While the whiff of revolution may have been in the air, it is also true to say that Carnaby Street was more about racking up huge profits from teenage trends, than a reflection of some creative youth culture. The "beat boom" was largely managed by the rich and dissolute sons of the Establishment, who, because of the cancellation of National Service, which would have previously seen them as officers in the Guards, were free to manipulate (mostly working class) musicians, who were ignorant of the ways of Tin Pan Alley.

The "Paris riots" demonstrate the reality effectively. Though the students on the streets brought fear to De Gaulle, the leaders would later admit that they had no plan for "after the revolution was won". The whole affair was defeated as much by its own lack of purpose as it was by De Gaulle's actions.

In retrospect, whilst seeming to be a grand uprising of youth, "the Sixties" was really an opportunity for the Establishment to re-order the way in which it controlled dissidence. It was allegedly about "Freedom" but, for most, it was actually an exercise in fairly cynical manipulation. Even the Troubles – ignited by a desire for Civil Rights - soon morphed into the generational struggle for unity and republicanism.

What I am suggesting, I suppose, is that the impact of the sixties is more highly lauded nowadays than it was obvious to us at the time. So, if my life near Liverpool, of all cities, was relatively untouched by "flower power", what of Kilkee?

I remember one afternoon in the summer of 67, one of us (ok, it was me!) had the idea to pick a few of Timothy McInerney's lovingly tended flowers from the beds in front of the Hydro, stick them in our hair, and march into the lounge singing "San Francisco."

When we did so, we could not keep our faces straight, and neither could most of the guests. The whole "Sixties" thing was so remote from the reality of West Clare that we came across like children let loose with the dressing up box. And, in essence, that is what we were. Being in Kilkee, in 67, gave us permission to be ourselves – which took away from us, and our parents, the pressure of our being "teenagers".

I have already suggested that in those years, Kilkee felt much more remote than it would do today. Communications were slower and less reliable –whether transport, mail, the telephone system or the media in general. What happened in Dublin – never mind the UK or the USA – was definitely happening "somewhere else". For many, in all age groups, that was part of the attraction of the place.

I was in Kilkee when the Troubles erupted, in mid August 1969, and I could show you the place on the pavement, between the Irish House and Egan's bar, where I unfolded the Evening Herald and saw the banner headline: "Belfast in Flames"; I had had a similar experience a year before, when the evening paper told me that Soviet tanks had rolled into Czechoslovakia. Both these major events were revealed to me the day after they happened, even the conflagration in the North, less than 250 miles away – which would be unthinkable in this 'connected' age.

Later, of course, communications progressed. I saw Richard's Nixon's resignation speech live from the White House in August 1974, in the television lounge at the Marine Hotel – which was the same venue when I watched the Live Aid concerts in July 1985 – by which time Kilkee *did* feel "part of the worldwide event".

It is an interesting facet of my ongoing relationship with the town that Kilkee was my location when these major events happened and my recollection of them is forever linked with the place.

However, in the sixties, there is no denying that Kilkee felt like a place apart, which was, of course, part of its attraction.

Like most of rural Ireland at that time, even where a façade of "modernism" had been applied, under the surface remained a very simple, conservative, and unchanging approach to life.

Certainly, in Kilkee, there was no "fast lane" in which teenagers could experiment and take risks. It had built its reputation as a family holiday resort on the fact that all the family would be comfortable there, and the children would be "safe". That "safety" was often taken to refer to the nature of the sheltered strand for swimming, but it actually covered the type of holiday and the closeness of all generations in enjoying their time there.

If I have achieved anything in this memoir, I would hope to have communicated the fact that this was an era in which families happily holidayed together, perhaps the last era when that happened. There was no retreat to computer game, iPad, mobile phone, or iPod, and though, as teenagers, we had the freedom each day to go off together, without our parents, - geographically, and, I suspect, philosophically, - we could not get far away from them. Whilst today's teenagers may see that as a negative, (and maybe, in our sulkier moments, we did too, at the time!), in retrospect, there is a happiness to be found in the memories of good times shared, and the closeness forged between family members released from every day routine.

Nowadays there is a rush to paint the Ireland of these times as repressive, grey, and generally awful. However, while it cannot, and should not, be denied that in many ways the State treated its most vulnerable citizens appallingly in those years, it is also fair to say, if balance is to be applied, that whilst ignorance could lead to awful tragedy, it could also lead to a kind of simple bliss.

There is always an opposite and equal reaction, and, whilst a paternalistic state which was often heartless cannot be defended, the more positive effect was a country in which simplicity still existed, and where hospitality, neighbourliness, and what we would call "simple pleasures" could bring much joy, at least to some, and for part of the time, despite much formalised hypocrisy.

This was clearly true in rural Ireland, but to be fair, at this time, the style and atmosphere of Dublin, similarly, still owed far more to its own history from the 30s and 40s, than its later pretensions to be a cosmopolitan European Capital. I suppose Dublin, like Kilkee, has had to measure how much to change and how much to conserve – and that's not always been a smooth process!

So the difference between the Pale and the West was perhaps not as wide as it is these days – but Kilkee could still feel a lot further than 187 miles from Anna Livia.

"Sophisticated" was not a word easily applied to Kilkee in the mid sixties. Then again, the folk who came back to the town year after year were not seeking a "sophisticated" holiday – whatever that might have meant. Indeed, I suspect many were seeking just the opposite. The joy of Kilkee was that you knew what to expect, and that the town, and its people, never tried to be something they were not. If it wasn't sophisticated, it was certainly authentic, and there was great pleasure to be had in going to a "real" place for your holiday, rather than to somewhere which was a confection, thought up for the purpose of earning tourist dollars and pounds.

At this distance, such a description may sound rather dismissive of Kilkee and what it offered. It is meant to be anything but.

I mentioned earlier that my delight in Kilkee and the times I spent there was partly down to timing. What Kilkee offered and what I wanted, or needed, matched perfectly in 1966, and continued to do so for many years after.

I was not a teenager of particularly sophisticated tastes. I liked, and still do prefer, simplicity and quietude – and Kilkee provided a match to those preferences.

So the fact that Kilkee matched my needs is one explanation of my infatuation with the town. There was also the fact that I felt comfortable there. I liked its streets, its architecture, the demeanour of its people – local and visitors; I loved the sense of space, freedom, and nature given by its sea, its cliffs, its rocks and hills. As you would expect from a favourite holiday place, it was very much a place in which I wanted to be.

It has to be said that, in the fifteen years or more I visited Kilkee on an annual basis, I was blessed with amazingly good weather – in Summer, Spring and Autumn – and the memory of sunshine and blue skies clearly paints a good picture. I don't think I've experienced more than a dozen wet days in Kilkee in my life, so my recollections are brightly lit in more ways than one.

I tend to think that it was the simplicity of Kilkee which led to the power of its effect on us.   It was different to home in every sense, and it felt like it – in styles and fashions. It was ensconced in what were at the time the traditional values of Irish life – Church and Family. If you wanted a holiday to give you a break from the pressures of every day life, Kilkee was your only man. It was escapism of the best kind.

In addition, for me as an only child, the feeling of being part of an "extended" family for three or four weeks every year was attractive. I never felt lonely or lonesome as an only child, I knew no other upbringing, but I did enjoy the companionship in Kilkee, and the change from school friends and school routines for a few weeks. It was, I suppose, socially refreshing.

Furthermore, I had a chance to partially "re-invent" myself on holiday, as we all do to some extent, and some of the confidence I achieved in being slightly different to my "home" self, was carried over to my every day existence when I returned home.

As I explained at length, the experience of the Hydro Ballroom was not something I could ever have accessed anywhere else. It contributed greatly to my development as a teenager. All of these positives gained from my times in Kilkee are, of course, common holiday benefits – they are among the reasons why we take a holiday – and Kilkee provided them perfectly for me.

I don't hanker for the times when I was fourteen years old, and, as I've said, I am well aware that Kilkee needs to develop - to maintain its population and its chances of prosperity. So, when I revisit Kilkee I don't go looking for ghosts, I don't expect it to be unchanged, nor do I wonder if I will recapture the feelings I had there as a child. I am delighted at the progress being made by the Loop Head community in terms of sustainable tourism – perhaps the nearest approach to holidaymaking in the sixties which is possible today.

However, it is an indisputable fact that this is a place which I knew well and which knew me well when I was a teenager. Its familiarity echoes those times, its memories are redolent of those far off days.

I am lucky enough to still have a number of friends from my schooldays. We don't live near each other and we see each other irregularly, but, when we meet up, we could be those same school boys travelling to school together all those years ago. There is an ease and a comfort in our relationship which is effortless and almost unconscious in its execution. We *know* each other, it seems like we always have.

I suppose that is how I feel about Kilkee.

The place has known me for a long time, and first welcomed me in my formative years. When I walk along the Strandline, or out to the Diamond Rocks, I cannot pretend to be someone I am not. These places know me of old, they know who I am – and, as a human being, such continuity and affirmation are invaluable to me. They give perspective and context, reassurance and comfort. Why would I not love the place?

Maureen Haugh perhaps best personified that feeling in a very real way. Over the years, as a boy, as a student, as a young adult, and as a man in middle age with a family, I could enter that cabin overlooking the Duggerna Reef and be assured of the same, calm and warm welcome: "Well, hello, John! How are you – and how is your mother?" I may have changed, and Kilkee may have changed, but that familiar welcome was still based on who I had been and what the town had been in my youth. Whatever we have been through in our later lives, it always seems that Kilkee recognises and welcomes the child we once were.

Kilkee and its people are what they are; they do what they do best – which is to welcome people, share the beauty of the place with them, and engender an almost overwhelming feeling of well being and relaxation. It is an experience which is addictive and pulls many people many miles, throughout their lives, to enjoy it again and again.

It is not so much a case of trying to repeat the holidays of our youth as seeking to recapture the joy they brought, and to remind ourselves how lucky we were to have discovered this beautiful place when we were young enough to appreciate fully all it had to offer.

There may be more houses now in Kilkee, there may be wilder weekends, there may be more exotic places around the world which are now within our reach, compared to those simple days of the sixties, but Kilkee still exists within our hearts and minds. That may seem to be an exaggerated claim – but any time a picture of the town is posted online, or a blog is written, or a news article shared – the reaction is always the same, from people of all ages and in all parts of the world, and in large numbers: "Oh God, I loved going to Kilkee; I wish I was there now!"

Geographically Kilkee may be far away from us, but, emotionally it is forever in our hearts – it is part of our make up, partly responsible for the way we are, even though we may not have been there physically for decades. Everybody we meet, every place we go, every experience we undergo leaves its mark on us and becomes ingrained in who we are. For those of us who were touched by Kilkee in our formative years, its influence is always there, no matter how subliminally.

What Kilkee gave us was a simple and uncomplicated joy, which would last a lifetime. It provided a reservoir of positivity and optimism into which we could dip to offset the darker moments in life, to remind ourselves that, sometimes, life could be more than just bearable, more than good – that, sometimes, it could be almost beautifully perfect. That's what Kilkee gave to those of us who were lucky enough to fall head over heels in love with the place.

We remember the seaweed, the turf smoke, the feel of the wind, the dazzle of the sun on the waves, the sound of the rollers on the strand, the taste of the salt on our lips. All of this ensured we were connected to Kilkee by all of our senses. And this connection was heightened by our being on holiday, by friendships established, by the re-creation of our spirit – all focused by the limited time we had there. We were safe in being ourselves, at ease with our surroundings, celebrating being uncomplicated humans – at least for a defined period.

In the context of time and place, Kilkee was not "magical" – it was as real as London, New York, Limerick or our own towns. Its effect on us as visitors may have seemed like magic, but luckily for us, its reality was exactly what we needed.

Sitting on the wall, we were not just watching Kilkee, we were watching our own lives – luckily, without realising it. Being able to recognise that fact a lifetime later only adds to the pleasure we felt at the time. Then, I was just a kid, having the time of my life, following my "Kilkee routine" without too much thought.

However, the Ballroom, the Hydro, the pitch and putt, the Diamond Rocks, and sitting on the wall – they all left their mark on me, their influence can be detected in my adult character, carved like Ryder Haggard's initials, in the Edmond Point of my personality!

There were many times in Kilkee when I wished the moment could be never ending – sitting at the Diamond Rocks – alone and wrapped in surroundings which seemed timeless, pausing on the pitch and putt to look out towards George's Head, pushing open the door into Egan's to receive a warm welcome, easing my way into the Hydro Lounge after hours of dancing in the Ballroom, watching shooting stars over the strand, walking along Marine Parade just bursting with the joy of being there, feeling the surge of familiarity as the car headed down O'Curry Street on each new arrival, watching a young child, all concentration and excitement, holding its parent's hand as it walked in the footsteps of a thousand children along the top of the sea wall. They were precious moments because, without needing to think about it, or even acknowledge the fact, we had an innate understanding that they were perfect, they were part of the reason for being on earth in the first place.

And now I find myself thinking the same about this memoir. Revisiting Kilkee, walking its streets and strand again, scrambling over half remembered rocks, passing once familiar faces on the Strandline, I have reminded myself how glorious it all was, how much I enjoyed it, and how important the old place remains in my heart and mind – and I don't really want to stop. Nobody ever wanted to leave Kilkee!

There is a world in which Kilkee is merely one of a string of west coast resorts, struggling to make progress against the tide of tourist history, with a third of its residents unemployed, and, according to the 2011 census, 71% of its housing stock, including holiday homes, uninhabited, eighteen pubs having closed in the past decade, and at least two of its major hotels are either shut, or for sale.

These are facts, with which, as they say, you cannot argue.

But they do not tell the whole story, and a snapshot in time can be balanced against half a century of experience. In this memoir, I have tried to offset the cartoon view of the daytripper or weekender, with the empathy of one who has maintained a love of the town for a lifetime. If Kilkee and I are celebrating our Golden Wedding, you can take it that I am equally as aware of its faults as I am of its glories – but I also know which side of the balance weighs most heavily!

Tá anam I gCill Chaoi – there is a soul in Kilkee!

Kilkee has always been important to me – and I hope this memoir has done it justice - without deconstructing any of its special qualities. I can only re-emphasise that it is a personal view, based on the best of memory and reflection, and is not intended to hurt, misrepresent, or diminish in any way the town or its people.

Ultimately, Kilkee gave us happiness, and, hopefully, for most of us, that happiness endured.

I will always be grateful to the town and its people, they will always be in my heart.

Míle, míle buíochas!

207

208

Lightning Source UK Ltd.
Milton Keynes UK
UKHW022046111220
374997UK00012B/2626